Talking with the Clay

*The publication of this book was made possible
by generous support from the*
RICHARD LOUNSBERY FOUNDATION.

For the Pueblo People

Talking with the Clay

The Art of Pueblo Pottery

Text and Photographs by

Stephen Trimble

School of American Research Press   Santa Fe, New Mexico

SCHOOL OF AMERICAN RESEARCH PRESS
Post Office Box 2188, Santa Fe, New Mexico 87504-2188

DIRECTOR OF PUBLICATIONS: Jane Kepp
EDITOR: Tom Ireland
DESIGNER: Deborah Flynn Post
TYPOGRAPHER: Casa Sin Nombre
PRINTER: Dai Nippon Printed in Japan

Library of Congress Cataloging in Publication Data:

Trimble, Stephen A.
    Talking with the clay.

    Bibliography: p.
    Includes index.
    1. Pueblo Indians—Pottery. 2. Indians of
North America—Arizona—Pottery. 3. Indians of
North America—New Mexico—Pottery. I. Ireland, Tom. II. Title.
E99.P9T75 1987   738.2'08997   86-33902
ISBN 0-933452-15-2
ISBN 0-933452-18-7 (pbk.)

Cover: *Santa Clara melon jars by Helen Shupla (Richard M. Howard collection).* Frontispiece: *detail (kokopeli, the hump-backed flute player),
polychrome jar by Lois Gutierrez-de la Cruz, Santa Clara (Richard M.
Howard collection).*

Contents

Acknowledgments   ix

Introduction
    The People   1

1. Talking with the Clay: Technique   9

2. Mountain Villages: Taos and Picuris   31

3. The Red and the Black: Tewa Pueblos   37

4. Storytellers and Birds: Middle Rio Grande Pueblos   55

5. Clay Made from History: Acoma, Laguna, and Zuni   73

6. The Legacy of Sikyatki: Hopi   89

Conclusion
    One with the Clay: Economics and Tradition   103

Notes on Sources   109

Index   113

Acknowledgments

I COULD NOT HAVE done this book without the trust and patience extended by the School of American Research, particularly Jane Kepp and Jonathan Haas. For her good taste, creativity, and cooperation, I thank the School's designer, Deborah Flynn Post. Michael Hering, director of the Indian Arts Research Center at SAR, helped in many ways.

Rick Dillingham and Richard M. Howard were generous with their time, knowledge, editorial criticism, and collections. Al Anthony, Robert Breunig, Laurie Davis, Andrea Fisher, and Alfonso Ortiz suggested potters to me. Andrea Fisher generously allowed me to photograph pottery in the Case Trading Post at the Wheelwright Museum, Santa Fe. Barbara Babcock shared her storyteller research and gave me permission to quote from her work. I also thank Ann Marshall at the Heard Museum, Phoenix, and Ann Hedlund and Art Wolf at the Millicent Rogers Museum, Taos. Jane Kepp and Tom Ireland kept me on the right track editorially, and Rebecca Staples offered additional useful comments. Linda Montoya made the black-and-white prints of my photographs.

Two people deserve special thanks. In 1984, my friend Robert Breunig transformed my career when he asked me to work on the slide program "Our Voices, Our Land" for the Heard Museum. And the idea for this book came from conversations with Maria Sauter.

I extend my apologies to the many fine potters I have neglected. I have tried to provide a fair sampling of both well-known and beginning artists, diverse styles, and major families. But I made no effort to document every active potter in each pueblo.

Most of all, I thank the many potters and Pueblo people, whose generosity, artistry, and courage made this book possible and my life infinitely richer. It was an honor to meet them and make this book for them.

S. T.
Jaconita, New Mexico

The People

A T PICURIS PUEBLO, cradled by green forest in New Mexico's Sangre de Cristo Mountains, when the village prepares to replaster its adobe church, the workers make a pile of plastering dirt next to the old mission. The sharp edges and faded designs of broken pottery glint in this soil—potsherds from generations past about to be mixed into mud plaster and become a part of a church that will be used by generations into the next century.

At Taos, the elders ask a young potter to make a bowl for ceremonial use in the kiva. They reject her first effort; it looks too new. They want one blackened with smoke, and so she refires her bowl, smudging it black. The elders are satisfied.

Isleta Pueblo, south along the Rio Grande, celebrates its feast day every year on the fourth of September. After mass, the people carry a carved image of Saint Augustine in procession around the plaza. Near the shrine on the far side of the square, where the saint will be honored, a Pueblo woman offers food to the carved *santo*. Under the approving eyes of the village priest, she walks to the head of the procession with a pottery bowl of steaming chile stew and wafts the steam toward the saint's unmoving face.

Left, *Anasazi pot sherds*; above, *Zuni Olla Maidens, Inter-Tribal Ceremonial Parade, Gallup.*

"We come into this world with pottery and we are going to leave the earth with pottery," says Acoma Pueblo potter Dolores Garcia: Acomas are bathed in a pottery bowl at birth and buried with pottery when they die. Pottery is a tradition, but it is also a part of contemporary life. It is art—vital, everyday art—both a creation and a symbol of the Pueblo people.

The Pueblos are one people and many people. They share a way of life, a world view, and a landscape. They speak half a dozen languages and live in more than thirty villages scattered across a 350-mile crescent of land from Taos, New Mexico, to the Hopi mesas in northern Arizona. Their immediate ancestors lived in an even vaster area from central Utah to deep in northern Mexico and from Nevada to Texas.

Pottery comes from the earth. It is made with clay, painted with minerals and plants, shaped with stones and gourds. Pueblo artists take these pieces of the land and make pottery, and in doing so they create a bond between land and people. Hopi-Tewa potter Dextra Quotskuyva speaks of trying to incorporate the whole universe—the earth and the sky and human lives—into the designs of her pottery. A Taos man says, "The story of my people and the story of this place are one single story. No man can think of us without thinking of this place. We are always joined together."

The land is where we begin.

The Pueblo Landscape

Archaeologist Erik Reed defined the Southwest as the territory between Durango, Mexico, and Durango, Colorado, and between Las Vegas, Nevada, and Las Vegas, New Mexico. Within this enormous division of the continent lie the southern end of the Rocky Mountains, the deserts of the Basin and Range country, and the high, rocky tablelands of the Colorado Plateau.

Two great rivers drain this land: the Colorado and the Rio Grande. Both flow south from the Rockies: the Colorado to the Pacific at the Gulf of California, the Rio Grande to the Gulf of Mexico. The Colorado River cuts through the plateau to which it gives its name in deep canyons, climaxing at the Grand Canyon, westernmost boundary of the Pueblo world. The Rio Grande flows south from the San Juan Mountains of Colorado through New Mexico in a north-south line with only a few gentle curves. In the northernmost part of New Mexico, the river runs in a dark and narrow gorge. Between Taos and Santa Fe, the Rio Grande passes between the two southernmost ranges of the Rocky Mountains: the Jemez Mountains on the west and the Sangre de Cristo Mountains on the east.

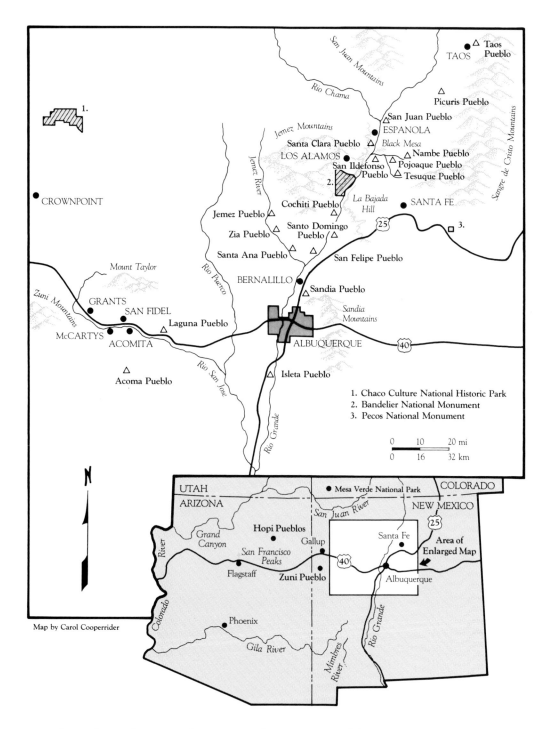

1. Chaco Culture National Historic Park
2. Bandelier National Monument
3. Pecos National Monument

| 0 | 10 | 20 mi |
| 0 | 16 | 32 km |

Map by Carol Cooperrider

Away from the river, the two northernmost pueblos sit in spectacular settings: Taos, right up against the Sangre de Cristos; and Picuris, within the mountains. A little north of Española, the Rio Grande Gorge opens out into a rich floodplain, and from here south lie the other so-called Rio Grande pueblos. Eight stand near the main channel of the river: a northern cluster in the rift between the mountains (San Juan, Santa Clara, San Ildefonso) and a set of southern villages where the river flows out into desert basins (Cochiti, Santo Domingo, San Felipe, Sandia, and Isleta).

Pojoaque, Nambe, and Tesuque lie on eastern tributary creeks of the big river just north of Santa Fe. Santa Ana, Zia, and Jemez pueblos fringe the southern mesas of the Jemez Mountains on the Jemez River, tributary to the Rio Grande from the west.

West of the Rio Grande Valley near Albuquerque, angular desert mountain ranges give way to long lines of mesas cut through by squared-off canyons faced with cliffs of red and golden sandstone. Here and there rises a small island of mountain forest. This is the Colorado Plateau, the prehistoric Pueblo heartland, home to the Pueblo ancestors, the people called Anasazi.

On the Rio San José just off Interstate 40, Laguna is the first living pueblo encountered on the trip westward. Farther west—farther from the highway, farther from water, and farther from familiar worlds—lie the pueblos of Acoma and Zuni. Acoma, the "sky city," perches securely on top of a mesa south of Mount Taylor. Zuni Pueblo stands at the western foot of the Zuni Mountains on the edge of the sweeping and open desert grassland known as Navajo country. Finally, deep in the remote plateaus of north-central Arizona, lie the Hopi villages—except for two far-flung farming communities, all built on or near three arid and rocky mesas that jut like ships' prows over the plains leading away to the Grand Canyon and the San Francisco Peaks.

Sacred arrays of mountains, lakes, and mesas bound the world of every pueblo. The land is stark, as sharply delineated as life and death. The health of each pueblo depends on this land, on the rain that nourishes the fields, and on the ceremonies and dances that ensure adequate rainfall. The people plan their ceremonial calendar around the seasons for planting and harvest, guided by the sun. Solstices are times of extremes; equinoxes are times of order and balance. The Pueblo world, both mundane and spiritual, reflects these unequivocal dualities: winter and summer, solemn ritual and outrageous clowning, right and wrong, Father Sun and Mother Earth.

Pueblo pottery captures this refined sense of order, opposition, and balance. Black on white. Paired figures. Symmetry. When potters sit down to outline a design on a slipped and polished vessel, they see with a perspective honed by every other aspect of their existence. Pueblo people start with the boundaries of their world and then work toward the center in reaching understanding. They do the same with their pottery. Over and over again, the potters say that they let the clay form itself to whatever shape it wants, without their conscious control; then they simply paint in the design dictated by the form.

Piñon smoke and sun-warmed adobe, Taos Pueblo.

Pueblo: Village, Language, People

An Acoma potter is an Acoma Indian, a Pueblo Indian, and linguistically, a Keresan. A Picuris person is Pueblo, Tanoan, and speaks Northern Tiwa. No wonder a common question from travelers in the Southwest is, "Who are the Pueblo Indians?" These native people live in stone and adobe towns, farm nearby fields, and share distinctive arts and religion. The word *pueblo* means "village" in Spanish and refers both to the towns and to the people. But many subdivisions exist within this greater category.

Language, the anthropologist's favorite method for distinguishing between cultures, proves both useful and confusing in the case of the Pueblos. The Hopis speak a language related to that spoken by Great Basin tribes farther west. Their nearest Pueblo neighbors, the Zunis, speak a language considered unique but perhaps distantly related to some Californian Indian dialects. Acoma, Laguna, and the Rio Grande pueblos of Zia, Santa Ana, San Felipe, Santo Domingo, and Cochiti speak Keresan, a language that also stands by itself. The rest of the Rio Grande pueblos speak Tanoan—also spoken by the Kiowas, Plains Indian people. But even among Tanoan speakers, substantial differences exist between the dialects of Northern Tiwa (Taos and Picuris); Tewa (San Juan, Santa Clara, San Ildefonso, Pojoaque, Nambe, and Tesuque); Towa (Jemez); and Southern Tiwa (Sandia and Isleta).

To further complicate matters, Pueblo social organization does not necessarily follow the lines of language groups: the Western Pueblos of Acoma, Laguna, Zuni, and Hopi often differ as a group from the Rio Grande Pueblos. When such confusing variety exists in people with whom we can talk, imagine the task of the archaeologist trying to untangle the story of the prehistoric Southwest.

Archaeologists speak of four main prehistoric Southwest peoples. The Mogollon lived in highlands across central Arizona and New Mexico and southward; the Anasazi dominated the Four Corners plateau country and the upper Rio Grande. The Mogollon and Anasazi disappeared as recognizable cultures after living here for about fifteen hundred years, but they live on in today's Pueblo people, their inheritors and descendants. Two other desert cultures, in southern Arizona, were neighbors rather than direct ancestors of the Pueblos (though some Hopi Water Clan people say otherwise).

The number of living pueblos is finite. In places, the Southwest was more densely populated in prehistoric times than it is today. Across the canyons and mesas in the Four Corners country lie thousands of ruined and abandoned villages.

We define these prehistoric groups by what we can excavate: villages, houses, jewelry, and more than anything else, pottery. Some archaeologists spend so much time analyzing pottery fragments (potsherds) that pottery almost becomes synonymous with culture.

Today we see pottery as art, but besides making beautiful pottery, prehistoric peoples made ceramic vessels as containers used for cooking, to carry water, and to store food safely from insects and rodents. Mogollon people first began depending on pottery instead of baskets about A.D. 200, and after another three centuries, potterymaking had spread across the Southwest. By about A.D. 500, the southwestern people had become farmers, nurturing fields of corn, squash, and beans. In the seventh century they began to decorate their pottery, painting whiteware and redware with black designs, then creating multicolored polychrome. In southern New Mexico around A.D. 1000, the Mimbres people, a group within the Mogollon tradition, painted some of the most artistically remarkable pottery in the prehistoric Southwest.

The Anasazi absorbed the Mogollon in prehistoric times, but abandoned the great towns of Chaco Canyon by the late 1200s, Mesa Verde and the San

Juan River drainage by 1300, and many other traditional homelands by 1450. For a century, archaeologists have puzzled over these facts. Each ruin remains irrevocably silent. But the people were not destroyed. They simply moved. Their descendants live in today's Pueblo villages.

Every modern pueblo has a set of stories about how its clans gathered from many places to come to the one place they should live and where they live today, the "center of the universe" for each people. Each clan had migrations to complete and depended on its religious leaders to announce when the time had come to move on. Oral traditions recognize many Mogollon and Anasazi ruins as ancestral sites.

Movement and change continued after the Spaniards came to the Pueblo world. The Europeans brought new diseases that decimated the Pueblo people. The western pueblos may have lost eighty percent of their population in the first century after contact with the Spanish. The Pueblo people have abandoned at least sixty-one villages since 1540, many because the population dropped too low for farming and proper ceremonial life to continue. For instance, the last seventeen Pecos Indians, the remnant of what once was New Mexico's largest pueblo, moved to Jemez in 1838.

After brutal religious persecution by the Spaniards, the Pueblos revolted in 1680 and exiled the Spanish from the Southwest until 1692, and permanently from Hopi. Many Rio Grande Pueblo people took refuge with the more isolated Hopis, and a village of Tewa-speaking people remains on First Mesa to this day. Keresan and Towa refugees founded Laguna in 1697. During this period, the Spanish banned pottery from burials, and as a result, little historic Pueblo pottery has survived.

Today, ancient traditions live on among the Pueblo people. They steadfastly protect their sacred ceremonies, keeping them secret from eyes of inadequate understanding when they feel that it's necessary. At the same time, they live in twentieth century America, and in so doing live with one more duality—the difficult search for a path between the old ways and the new. They borrow and incorporate many non-Indian ideas. They listen to their elders to make sure they remember the old ideas that give them strength.

Pottery helps to bridge the gap between worlds, springing from old ways but generating an income in a wage-based society. Pueblo potters carry on with the grace, intuition, and eloquence of their ancestors. The people build their designs—their "stories"—into their pottery. Along with the southwestern landscape and the traditions of a people who have lived here for thousands of years, each Pueblo pot carries with it a part of the potter's spirit—all joined together, people and place, in a "single story" embodied in clay.

CHAPTER ONE

Talking with the Clay: Technique

BLUE CORN SAYS of her fellow San Ildefonso potters, "Doing this potterymaking in the traditional way—with their hands without using a machine at all—it's really a miracle. To them and to me too." Young Hopi Tracy Kavena has learned pottery from her grandmother Rena. Her judgment: "It's harder than it looks."

This difficult miracle starts with nothing more than what most of us call dirt: with clay. Because it can be made of many kinds of minerals (usually hydrous aluminum silicate), geologists define clay ambiguously as a naturally occurring fine-grained material with "plastic properties." This phrase sums up clay's possibility for miracles. Wet it and shape it and fire it and "its particles soften and coalesce upon being highly heated and form a stony mass on cooling." Clay becomes pottery.

Left, *Bessie Namoki shapes a pot from yellow Hopi clay*; above, *Lois Gutierrez's polishing stones, Santa Clara.*

Picking Clay

Pueblo potters often speak of "picking" clay, as they would pick flowers. Clay is a gift from Mother Earth, and like all of her gifts, it is sacred. Potters pray before taking the clay; they make an offering of cornmeal, asking permission from Mother Earth to take part of her body to use for pottery to support themselves and their children. Hopi-Tewa Dextra Quotskuyva says, "You have to offer something in order to get it, you just don't go out there and dig, I want this, I want that. You just get the amount you are going to use."

Bernice Suazo-Naranjo, from Taos, has "learned to really respect the clay. And I think that comes natural because we are all raised in an environment so that we're in tune with nature. It's a cycle."

Not every woman still leaves behind a cornmeal offering when she digs clay, but all speak with reverence of their medium. Some potters keep special clay sources secret. At other pueblos, everyone uses the same clay pit. Young people search for new clays to experiment with. Old potters may cease making pottery altogether if their usual clay source disappears.

Digging clay is hard physical labor. Men often help their wives and daughters with this task, making it a family outing. Derek de la Cruz helps his wife, Santa Clara potter Lois Gutierrez, gather clay. He says, "If you look hard enough, you can find clay here and there all over the mountains, but you got to look for it. It doesn't just jump out at you. It's beautiful when you dig in it. The white clay looks like candy, white chocolate. When you're digging it, you don't want to stop, it feels so neat."

Potters have guessed that they spend half their time processing materials for potting—just preparing for the creative act. Once the lumps of rough clay have been brought home, the preparation begins. Nathan Youngblood of Santa Clara estimates that it takes twenty-four to thirty hours of work to mix up one cubic foot of clay.

The raw clay is dried before soaking and sometimes ground and sieved clean. One potter says that if you do not dry the clay, it will have a "rotting smell" when you soak it for long periods. Another explains that it will stay lumpy unless you dry it completely before soaking. While the clay soaks in washtubs or barrels, the potters change the water several times to purify the clay, dissolving out stray minerals. Once the clay is saturated, they sieve and sift out the impurities: stones, branches, and roots.

If potters use pure clay in shaping their vessels, the pots will crack as they dry and shrink, for the outside surface dries faster than the inside. The surface of the pot would look like the mud curls along a dry riverbed, or the pot would simply crack and disintegrate. Adding a stable *temper* of sand or finely

Pottery and drying clay in front of Jodie Chino's house in the "Sky City" of Acoma.

ground rock or potsherds makes for slower, more even drying, and over the centuries, Pueblo potters have refined their sense of exactly how much temper to use.

Preparing temper can be just as time consuming as picking clay. Northern Rio Grande Pueblo people temper their clay with ground volcanic ash and tuff, sometimes called "Pojoaque sand"; they have done so since 1200. Zia potters have used finely ground basalt for six centuries. And at Acoma, Laguna, and Zuni, the artists manufacture their temper by grinding old pottery sherds to add to fresh clay. Some clay at Taos, Picuris, and Hopi needs no added temper: it already contains the right amount of sand or gritty mica. When they go searching for clay, potters look for color first: they can adjust texture by tempering, but color can be altered only by slips, paints, and firing techniques.

Mixing the clay and temper is a crucial step. Santana Martinez of San Ildefonso calls it mixing the "dough," and finds it the hardest part of making pottery. Bernice Suazo-Naranjo and her husband Tito learned the technique by trial and error. Their first attempt at making Taos pottery with micaceous clay was a disaster—they collected a beautiful red clay, but it was mostly sand, and all Bernice's pots fell apart. Later they learned to recognize rich veins of fine clay, which was "just like striking gold." Dolores Garcia of Acoma felt she "had steel gloves on her hands" the first time she mixed clay. Now, after mixing the clay with her hands, she continues to wedge it with her feet—much easier. Juana Leno says that these days the Acomas have tender feet, and her family kneads their clay with tennis shoes on.

Occasional crises in the sources of temper occur. For instance, in response to Santa Clara's charging other Pueblo people to hike and fish in Santa Clara Canyon, Pojoaque closed off its sand quarries in 1968—temper sources that Santa Clara potters had used for forty years. It took a full season for the Santa Claras to find a new volcanic tuff deposit and readjust their clay mixture to perfection. Today the people of both Santa Clara and San Ildefonso pay Pojoaque Pueblo for the right to collect sand.

Experience teaches an instinctive certainty about the right consistency in the mix of water, clay, and temper. The most refined clays can be shaped immediately. Rougher clays become more workable with aging. Bernice Suazo-Naranjo keeps her coarse Taos micaceous clay in plastic bags for three to four months, aging it to a "wonderful plasticity." Once mixed, the clay not only smells good, but tastes good. Stella Shutiva's grandchildren sneak up behind her when she is working and take little pieces of Acoma clay to eat.

Men may help in the hard work of mixing clay or in painting, and today many men make fine pottery. Nambe-Pojoaque potter Virginia Gutierrez believes men make better potters than women: "They have more of an artistic ability." Stella Shutiva says, "Men are strong. They make big pots, pots shaped the way their bodies are shaped, narrow at the base and wider at the top. Women make pots that are plumped."

Traditionally, men did not shape pots. That was woman's work. In Alice Marriott's *Maria: The Potter of San Ildefonso*, Maria Martinez's mother taught her daughters, "It was the woman's part of living to hold things together. Men could build up or tear down houses and ditch banks; but women put clay and sand together to make pottery. That was part of a woman's life, to make things whole."

Today, both men and women potters "make things whole." Their art is integrated with their life. Maria's great-granddaughter Barbara Gonzales believes that "whenever an Indian gets involved with art they do it with their whole being—that's what makes the art unique." The past, the present, and the future all are captured and united in the act of making pottery.

The Selfish Clay

Rose Naranjo of Santa Clara says, "The clay is very selfish. It will form itself to what the clay wants to be. The clay says, I want to be this, not what you want me to be." The clay forms itself, but if the potter has "a good intention," is "one with the clay," the pot will please both the clay and the shaper. It will be an extension of the potter's spirit.

More than anything else, coiling defines Pueblo pottery: coiled pots are built by hand, never thrown on a wheel. Ernest Tapia of Santa Clara says, "If we use a wheel, that's not art. That's the white man's way. Too perfect. A woman can make anything, any kind of a shape with her own hands."

First the potter pats out a base from a cone of clay, much as she would pat out a tortilla or work with bread dough. If she plans a piece larger than palm sized, she will need a base known as a *puki* to support the growing coils. Only small pots and figurines are pinched from a ball of clay without coils or a puki. Potters used to make pukis from the broken bases of old pots. Today, they may use china plates, pie tins, cereal and salad bowls—anything that works. Hopi-Tewa potter Mark Tahbo sweeps a hand around his kitchen, indicating the bowls and dinnerware he uses as pukis, and says, "These are my wheels."

The potter pinches out a rim at the edge of the puki-supported clay foundation, then rolls a first coil of moist clay and presses it along the inside edge of the round base. Coil by coil—each coil about an inch in diameter—the potterymaker constantly turns the growing pot, maintaining just the right moistness of clay to ensure that new coils adhere, and the piece begins to rise. Constant kneading works out air bubbles that would ruin the pot in firing. Small vessels can be made complete—built up, smoothed, and shaped—and the potter can move right on to the next piece. Vessels large enough to approach the limits of the clay's physical strength must be made in stages, each section shaped to its final proportions and the base allowed to dry and strengthen before the next series of coils can be added. Robert Tenorio of Santo Domingo lets the base rest when the wall of his forming pot starts to "jiggle."

An energetic potter may shape twenty-five small bowls and jars in a day. A large piece may require a few hours to a full week of careful on-and-off work. Small pieces can be built up with straight sides, like buckets, then pushed out into the smooth curves of a jar or bowl. Santana Martinez even starts her plates this way.

Shaping and scraping roughs out the form. Pueblo people have long used potsherds or pieces of gourd rind for scrapers. Today they also use an assortment of coconut shells, tongue depressors, paring knives, wooden spoons, discarded eyeglass lenses, car windshield ice scrapers, can lids, and tops from candy, tobacco, and aspirin tins. Emma Mitchell of Acoma jokes that she and her mother and sister have kept Argentine corned beef companies in business because they use so many of their tins as scrapers and trimmers. Lillian Salvador has a special long-handled wooden tool for the inside of her Acoma wedding vases: "If I'm not careful I put a dent in it and there's no way to put your finger in there. So I put this in there and push it out."

The clay has a will of its own, and its shaper must be in tune with that will. "The clay knows when you're interested," says Rena Kavena. Dextra Quotskuyva "just waits on the clay. It seems to mold itself. It's the mood that you're in; your heart is right there with the clay." Blue Corn "does not make a pot just because I like it. I have to make a pot that will like me. And looks like it's talking to me, too. At the same time, I'm talking to that pot, too, or to the clay that I'm working with." Sometimes the pottery says to Tracy Kavena, "I'm just right. Don't mash me up. You might not like me but someone else will."

"So much of me goes into the pot," says Gladys Paquin of Laguna. "Even my thoughts are in the pot. I have to tell the pot how to be. The stubborn ones I give the okay to be that way. You have to realize which one wants to be and which one you should start over again."

Dora Tse Pe Peña of San Ildefonso believes, "If you're angry and if you are making pots with bitter feelings toward others or towards something, your pots will act accordingly." Jody Folwell of Santa Clara agrees: "My pieces start out somewhere deep down inside of me. I feel that physically I just make what comes out of me spiritually. The pieces seem to mold themselves. I never really mold them."

Some potters strive for thinner and thinner walls. Some prefer thicker, more substantial walls. Usually the scraper will smooth away all evidence of the coils. But for corrugated pottery, the artist leaves each coil visible and decorates it with rows of scallops and indentations made with her fingertips, the pointed metal tip of a can opener, or a carved juniperwood tool. Handles, lugs, and appliqued animal or corn sculptures are all added during shaping, with the clay still wet and pliable.

The possibilities of shape are infinite. A complex interaction between tradition, convention, and an artist's sensibilities makes the rules. Even at this stage, every pot is unique.

In the porch of his home at Santo Domingo on a sunny afternoon, Robert Tenorio builds a bowl from moist clay, coil by coil (left), scraping (bottom) and smoothing it (right) with tools cut from dried gourds.

Nancy Lewis sands her pottery in her house in the Hopi village of Sichomovi on top of First Mesa.

A Turn of the Sandpaper

To avoid cracks some clays require slow drying after shaping. Other clays can withstand sun-drying, or even a warm oven. Once the clay has dried, the potter refines or even resculpts the shape by sanding and scraping. No one says that sanding is her favorite part of the art. It is dirty, dusty, and tedious. It makes the worker sneeze. Even in winter, the rest of the family may insist that the potter sand outside. But in this laborious step, each piece achieves its final form.

In addition to the corncobs and chunks of rough lava rock or sandstone they have always used, potters now use metal tools, window screen, steel wool, or commercial sandpaper. They must take care not to sand the walls too thin and sand a hole right through a pot. Rims are particularly fragile, and a chipped or cracked rim on a large jar may mean that the whole neck must be taken off the dried pot, converting a jar into a wide-mouthed bowl.

Taos pots on Bernice Suazo-Naranjo's kitchen counter wait their turn to be sanded.

Sanding eliminates the ridge left at the top of the puki. Also, if the potter carved designs in the drying pot when it was leather hard, she refines the carving during sanding, again a delicate task. The artist creates a soft haze of pottery dust with her sandpaper. Gradually, a line of smooth undecorated forms accumulates on the table or floor nearby, looking more like sculpture than ceramics, all trace of the coiling process gone.

Throughout the drying and scraping phases, the potter watches for cracks and air bubbles. Minor imperfections can be repaired with fresh wet clay and by rubbing the pot with a wet cloth. Major flaws mean the pot must be broken and merged with the next batch of molding clay.

Bernice Suazo-Naranjo admits, "Sanding the sculptures is not the most joyous part of making the pottery, but sanding is very crucial for me because that's when I refine. Just the turn of your sandpaper will determine whether you have a very traditional pot or a very contemporary one."

*Belen Tapia polishes
a Santa Clara pot
freshly slipped with
"Tewa red" clay.*

Polishing with Heirlooms

Bessie Namoki holds out a smooth gray pebble: "A man from Second Mesa found this polishing stone at Awatovi Ruin and gave it to my mother, maybe in about 1937. We've been using it ever since. I don't know what I would do if I ever lose it."

Pueblo pottery can shine like river cobbles after a rainshower, but it does so not from glazed finish but from hand-rubbed polish. At Hopi, the unmodified pot can be polished, but in most pueblos a thin solution of clay called a slip is painted on, and while still damp, rubbed carefully with a polishing stone or a clean rag to achieve the lustrous final finish. Santa Clara potters make thicker pots now to allow for the increased pressure needed to achieve the high polish that buyers prefer. Gladys Paquin polishes her red- and white-slipped Laguna bowls with a stone: "Polishing puts a brightness and softness to it; with a rag it is rough."

Slips accomplish several things. They smooth the surface with a coating of finely ground clay; they add color; some contribute to turning the plant-derived paint black in firing; and they provide the base layer for polishing and a blank ground or "canvas" for painting or incising.

Acoma, Zuni, and the middle Rio Grande villages use white slip. The delicate, white "Cochiti slip" cannot be touched during polishing, but Robert Tenorio knows of nothing else that will turn his Santo Domingo paint black in firing. It takes many thin coats of the creamy white Cochiti slip to cover the pot, and each must dry before the next is applied. Today potters sit in front of their ovens with the heat on low, for the pot must be warm to absorb each layer of slip. In former times they sat by their fireplaces, keeping the pots turned toward the coals.

"Well, we just have magic!" say Emma and Dolores Lewis at Acoma to explain what makes their pots so white; they laugh and explain proudly that

Bessie Namoki slips a smoothed, sanded Hopi bowl.

they use so many layers of slip that their pots are not just white, but "white white." Blue Corn describes how hard it is to polish the white slip that forms the base for her San Ildefonso polychrome: "Everytime I stroked a polishing stone on it all that whole thing peels off. I did it carefully, very slowly, and finally that whole slip stuck on the pot."

Dextra Quotskuyva uses just one polishing stone, given to her by her mother, but her daughter Camille thinks another one is better. Many potters use several stones, each one suited to a particular task: rims, sides, fluting, or miniatures. Not everyone has an heirloom stone; some buy polishing stones in rock shops or pick up river pebbles. Potters look for old polishing stones in ruins, and treasure them when they find them. Barbara Gonzales jokes that polishing stones are "pet rocks."

The complex incising called *sgraffito* owes its name to an Italian term for the technique of carving through the polished slip to expose the color of the clay beneath. Pueblo potters call this technique "etching." After polishing, they sculpt three-dimensional scenes on the sides of "etched" pots, both before and after firing.

Particularly on burnished black and red Tewa pottery, polishing is crucial. At San Ildefonso, Maria Martinez and her sister Clara established an ideal in the early twentieth century. They could polish better than anyone, and as Maria's pots became a paragon, the family's high polish became a standard to meet. Polishing takes a precise touch: press too hard, scratch the slip, and you must sand it off and do the whole thing again. Belen and Ernest Tapia at Santa Clara judge artists by how many times they are willing to sand off the slip and start over to get it right. After polishing the slip once, potters may apply a layer of grease or lard and polish the pot a second time. This not only increases the shine but helps keep the clay slip from shrinking.

You must finish polishing while the slip is damp, or scratching is inevitable. Carnation Lockwood of San Juan takes the phone off the hook when she polishes to avoid interruption; if her friends try to call and repeatedly get a busy signal, they know "Carnation's polishing today." When Mary E. Archuleta and her sisters were growing up at Santa Clara, their mother, Margaret Tafoya, would give one of them her pot to keep polishing when someone came to buy pottery. Mary says, "We tried to do the best we can when we did that. We didn't want to let her down and let the pot dry out. It gave us a feeling of trust, of confidence. When I started doing my own pottery, I felt like I could do it already. Mom says, 'A pot might not be perfect, but the finish is what makes it.' "

The classic Tewa high polish: a jar by Dora Tse Pe Peña of San Ildefonso that combines the traditional water serpent with the glitter of micaceous slip, inlaid turquoise, and a sienna rim. (Mudd-Carr Gallery)

Hopi potter Bessie Namoki paints a rim line with a yucca brush and a sure hand.

Painting Stories

A slipped, polished pot gleams in the potter's hands. How does she decide what to do next?

Emma Mitchell lines up two or three pots and looks at each one, wondering which design to use, until she *knows*. Robert Tenorio does not plan: "Once I start my lines, after I paint the base lines, the design just comes to me. Just go with it and before you know it I will have a finished painted pot." Bernice Suazo-Naranjo leaves some of her Taos micaceous pots undecorated: their form is so exquisite they need no design. Others look too plain to her, and she carves her design before firing.

"The plants, the rocks, everything in the earth inspires you, and with me, everything seems to have life." Dextra Quotskuyva gets up from bed when she dreams about designs and she sketches what she has seen. Later, she paints them: "I enjoy the painting because I paint how I feel."

The legendary Hopi-Tewa potter Nampeyo taught her granddaughter Daisy Hooee to paint freehand, without using a pencil to trace the design on the pot.

Daisy learned by "watching her, watching her, watching her." Eighty years later, she still paints designs in her grandmother's style, as well as designs of her own inspired by prehistoric potsherds. "There's where we get the ideas, there's where we get the stories from."

Pueblo people paint their designs—their "stories"—with a combination of bold intuition and careful thoughtfulness. Many use brushes made from a dried yucca leaf chewed so that exactly the right number of fibers extends from the tip, usually from one to twelve. Often they will do the fine work with old-style yucca brushes and fill in with commercial brushes. Yucca lets them paint places that are difficult to reach with long-handled commercial brushes. Wayne Salvador was amazed at how his wife Lillian painted the inside of one deep Acoma jar: "You almost have to stand upside down to do something like that. That's how much patience they've got." Some potters work late at night. To save their eyes, others paint only by daylight. As Mary Archuleta points out, "Haven't you noticed how many potters wear glasses?"

Tracy Kavena tried commercial paintbrushes first, but Hopi paint ate away the hairs. Now she says she can make finer lines and longer strokes with yucca. "The yucca knows just what you want to do—it knows where you want to go with the paint. The paint that is already on the pot is like a magnet—the yucca goes right back to the right spot."

Mixing paint is another of the many preparatory steps every potter must attend to. Black paint usually comes from what the artists call wild spinach, or *guaco*, the boiled-down residue from Rocky Mountain beeplant and tansy mustard. It keeps for years, and turns to paint whenever mixed with water. At some pueblos, guaco acts as a binder when mixed with ground mineral pigment. If the mix is not exactly right, paint may flake off in firing or fail to turn dense black. Paint also must be free of lint and dust so it will go on smoothly.

Some potters cook only the leaves of the beeplant; others use the whole plant, roots and all. Others say that almost any plant will yield the same black paint base when boiled down to thick syrup. Santo Domingo potters mix sugar with their "spinach juice" so the paint will stick better on the white slip. Red and yellow paint come from ocher or iron-rich mineral pigments, ground rock, and clay. Some Zia potters use black mineral paint with no guaco binder.

A painter must be in the right mood. It takes concentration. Emma Mitchell says, "When the telephone rings, you take off for two or three minutes, and when you come back, it's not the same." If Robert Tenorio makes a mistake, "there's no way that I can erase it, so I usually expand the design, or turn it into something else, maybe add an extra petal or leaf." His spinach-juice paint sinks into the white slip of the Santo Domingo pots: "Sometimes I go over it twice so that I know where the lines are."

Isleta potter Stella Teller does her best work alone: "I can't talk and paint at the same time." But Stella Shutiva, her daughter Jackie, and a son-in-law who does easel paintings all paint together. When they get tired, they troop out to the living room "and watch the soaps on TV for a while," then go back to work. Noise does not bother Lillian Salvador: "I've got five children and they are always screaming, so I guess I'm used to it."

Each pueblo has a set of traditional designs, and each potter paints them in an individual way. In the old days, before Indian artists signed work, they had to be able to recognize their own piece in a large array of pottery after a ceremony. They did so by means of subtleties obvious only to them. In her classic 1929 book *The Pueblo Potter*, Ruth Bunzel tells of going into Polacca Trading Post at Hopi with a local woman. The Hopi potter and the trader could identify the makers of virtually all the larger pieces among the several hundred in the storeroom. Bunzel was impressed: to her less practiced eye, many looked discouragingly alike.

Every style has inexhaustible variations. Shape, polish, and painting all distinguish a potter's pieces. Even something as simple as corrugated Acoma whiteware varies from potter to potter. Stella Shutiva's pieces are instantly recognizable by the particular texture given them by her corrugating tool and their nearly complete corrugation from top to bottom.

Pueblo people respect the old designs, but a fine potter cannot help putting her own stamp on them. Gladys Paquin says that her customers "tell me they all look different. I say, 'Yes, I'm not a machine.' "

Anthropologists sometimes lament this unending personal nuance. Ruth Bunzel speaks of the "problem" of variability within a given style. To the potters, however, variability in design is not a problem but the mark of each person's gift. It is art.

Baking the Potteries

Rose Naranjo calls firing "Judgment Day." After all the work of making pottery, Pueblo potters carry it outside, carefully build a fire of wood or manure, an outdoor kiln to be used just once, and take the ultimate risk of potterymaking—"baking their potteries." A gust of wind at the wrong time can drop the temperature and make a pot explode. Air bubbles in the clay can also make a pot "pop." Or a piece of manure falling onto the polished slip can smudge the pot with "fire clouds."

Even the most experienced women find a successful firing exciting and satisfying. Virginia Duran, at eighty-seven no longer potting, speaks with warmth of coming back to a firing after the ashes have burned down and seeing her Picuris pots poking through, "very pretty."

Bernice Suazo-Naranjo says, "When you lose a pot, you lose yourself. Sometimes you have a special feeling for a pot and you hate to fire it because you are so afraid it will break, but that's part of the beauty of firing outdoors. You have got to learn to cope with it. I like the idea that not everything is going to survive, because that's the way it is—part of being a potter."

Pueblo people build a kiln from scratch each time they ground-fire their pots, usually behind their house in a flat, protected place where they always fire. A grate a few inches off the ground supports the pots and leaves room for kindling underneath. Slabs of bark, juniper wood, and cakes of cow and sheep dung make up the main fire. Pieces of broken pottery, tin, flattened stovepipe, old bedsprings, and automobile shock absorbers shield the pots from the burning fuel. Santana and Adam Martinez complain of a new problem: cheaply made New Mexico license plates that melt onto the pots when they use them in their firings.

Stella Teller protects her figurines in tin cans that she gets from the Isleta school cafeteria; her large figures fit perfectly in pumpkin cans. Virginia Gutierrez fires her polychrome pieces in army surplus ammo cans or between two old children's wagons joined together into a box. "Sometimes I go to the dump and I find little containers that I can use like that. My husband looks at them and says to me, 'Where in the world have you been!'"

At Hopi, potters prefer sheep dung for firing, which they buy from enterprising Navajos who come to the mesa tops to sell it. Tracy Kavena's little girls asked her why she smelled so strong when she came in from firing. She told them, "That's the smell of money." Now whenever she fires, her daughters announce, "Mommy smells like money." Tracy's grandmother Rena reminds her to wear her oldest clothes for firing, in case she can't wash out the smell. At San Juan, Carnation and Bill Lockwood can hear their neighbors' doors slamming meaningfully on days when they stoke up their cow-chip fires.

Firing, like every step in the art, is sacred, and risky enough that even some of the less traditional people will make an offering before lighting their fires. Some potters use a firing ground blessed by a medicine man—a secret and sacred place.

A kiln is built with great care, sometimes with a barricade to shield the fire from the wind. Firing days are dry and calm; a hot, clean fire is critical. Potters try to fire at dawn in summer, when the air is still and cool. On hot summer days, says Mary Archuleta, "If we're a little bit late, we suffer. Firing really takes everything out of you." To completely dry out the earth, some potters build a small fire the night before.

They tend the firing until they know enough time has passed, then let it burn down, perhaps peeking into the fire to determine when the glowing, red-hot pots are done. Some pots must be removed at precisely the right time to prevent overfiring, which turns them dull. Mary Archuleta says "you have to be an expert with a pitchfork" to remove the pots and their racks.

With a good draft and plenty of oxygen throughout the process, most firings will burn clean. Zia potter Elizabeth Medina starts her fire with sheep dung, letting it smudge the pots, and then adds cow chips, stoking up the fire to burn off the smudges. Damp manure will turn Acoma pots blue instead of the desired white. To achieve the lustrous black surface so famous at Santa Clara and San Ildefonso, towards the end of firing potters smother the fire with fine horse manure, preventing oxygen from reaching the pots and creating a reducing atmosphere—and considerable smoke. In the reducing fire the

At Zia, Elizabeth Medina fires her pottery with a combination of sheep and cow manure, protecting the pots from fire smudges with old bedsprings and auto shock absorbers. When the firing is complete, she quickly dismantles the "kiln" and removes the finished pots for cooling.

oxygen-depleted oxide of iron forms instead of the red, oxygen-rich iron oxide, and the surface turns black. Ashes heaped on the manure keep the heat and smoke in even longer and prevent thermal shock.

Everyone hates to hear the sound of a pot "popping"—going off like "a bomb." Dora Tse Pe Peña says of her mother, Candelaria Gachupin of Zia, "If a pot cracks or a piece of it pops off in the firing or it just pops to pieces, she simply says, 'Well, you weren't meant to be.' When I'm firing and a pot pops, I get upset. The girls tell me, 'Mom, don't let Grandma hear you say that.' Many times, even before the firing, during the polishing or some step before the firing, it just doesn't do well. And I redo it and I redo it and it does not come out well. I know it wasn't meant to be. And maybe I should leave it at that point, but I keep trying, I keep trying, and I don't say, 'You weren't meant to be,' I just say, 'Hey you better be!' "

Emma Mitchell "doesn't feel bad about the pots we lose in firing because we reycle the ones that blew up in the fire. We use it as temper and it just goes right back into the clay." Bernice Suazo-Naranjo believes, "To me there is a beauty in losing a few pots, there is a beauty in doing the procedure, of going through the whole old traditional way."

Some people believe that firing problems can mean something bad is going to happen in the family. Rondina Huma at Hopi went through a time of "not getting good firing." One of her aunts died soon after, and "then it started firing okay again."

Nearly every potter has a few cracked pots in her home, pieces she cannot sell for a good price. All feel great affection for them. Candelaria Gachupin told her daughter that pots "are like people. We people have imperfections, do we destroy them because they are blind or deaf or have lost a limb? No, we don't destroy them. She told me that pots are the same way. You don't destroy a pot because it has an imperfection. You love it as much as you would a perfect pot."

Shortcutting the Traditions

Daisy Hooee lectures young potters, "Nowadays they want everything easy. But I tell them, if you make them with the commercial clay how can you tell that story? There's no story on it."

Even if you believe that commercial shortcuts do not make the potteries "lose their stories," shortcuts may or may not work. Robert Tenorio of Santo Domingo made contemporary stoneware before he made traditional Pueblo pottery. When he began the transition to the old Santo Domingo methods, he experimented with combinations of new and old techniques, but they didn't work together. Electric kilns burned off his spinach-juice paint and turned the white slip red or terra-cotta. The Cochiti slip would not stick to commercial clay. Neither Zia white, Acoma white, Laguna white, nor Jemez white turned the spinach juice black; only Cochiti white seemed to work. And he found that if he made up a design, it usually turned out to be some other pueblo's design. The old ways work in concert: every step depends on the others.

Each pueblo has worked out the combination of materials and techniques that makes its pottery distinct, and yet today, all the pueblos exist as part of a much larger world. Intermarriage between tribes and with Anglos is common. A potter may have parents from two different pueblos and be raised in a third. Navajo, Apache, or Plains Indian people may marry into a pueblo: do they then make Pueblo pots? More and more artists flirt with commercial clay or paint, send their pots off to town to be fired in an electric kiln, or paint commercially molded pots. Helen Cordero knows that "Grandma Clay doesn't like it" if Cochiti pots are taken to the big electric kiln in Albuquerque. Dora Tse Pe Peña says that kiln-fired pots "lose their meaning." What is tradition? Where does it begin and where does it end? Grace Medicine Flower says of her Santa Clara miniatures, "Now they call this contemporary; years from now they may call this traditional."

Perhaps more than anything, it comes down to the way the pottery *feels*—a feeling that has to do with the potter's intent. All ethical potters agree that they must be honest, that they must tell the truth about their materials. The pottery communicates much of this truth by itself.

Dextra Quotskuyva makes some pots with minimal painted designs. She "hopes people are able to touch it, have the feeling that there's something there, instead of just looking."

An Albuquerque psychiatrist tells his patients to buy Pueblo pottery and feel it. He doesn't know just why, but it makes them (and him, when he feels his own Pueblo pottery) feel better when they do. Santa Clara potter Jody Folwell suggests why: "There is so much incredible goodness that comes out of the pueblos and out of the people. It exists there a hundred times more so than in any other community. Anything that comes out of those villages has that particular power—spiritual power. So it's a very exciting kind of a feeling, always to be able to pick up a piece and say I love this piece. I'm going to take it home. Because that's where all of that power exists then."

CHAPTER TWO

Mountain Villages: Taos and Picuris

A T THE EASTERN BOUNDARY of the Pueblo world, the Sangre de Cristo range of northern New Mexico, the sun rises over high peaks at dawn, and the mountains glow blood red at sunset. At this frontier of Pueblo village life stand Taos and Picuris. Taos looks up to Pueblo Peak, where Blue Lake, most sacred of all Taos holy places, nestles high in spruce and fir. Picuris people live *in* the mountains. They say they dwell in a "hidden valley: the only way to get to Picuris is to climb a hill." Mountains dominate their settings as at no other pueblos. The people of Taos and Picuris also share distinctive ceremonies, dress, close historic relations with nomadic hunting tribes, and pottery.

The Tender Mica

Taos and Picuris use clay from their mountains. Instead of weathering from the sandstones and shales of deserts and plateaus, here the clay decays from ancient Precambrian gneiss and schist, rich in mica. This mineral peels off in glittery sheets of silver and gold, and its grittiness gives most Taos and Picuris clays enough leavening to require no additional temper.

Left, *Virginia Romero of Taos*; above, *glittering micaceous Picuris pottery (School of American Research collection).*

Virgina Duran of Picuris and one of her well-used bean pots.

Two elderly women, Virginia Duran of Picuris and Virginia T. Romero of Taos, embody the pottery traditions of these pueblos. They live twenty miles from each other, work in different styles, and speak with a friendly rivalry. Virginia Duran says Taos people learned how to make pottery from Picuris people: "The Taos people pick it up from here; it's not their job. Picuris pots are thin, not heavy like Taos."

Over at Taos, Virginia Romero speaks proudly of never losing a pot in firing from the time she started making pottery in 1919. Years ago, Virginia Duran asked her how this could be. Mrs. Romero demonstrated her firing methods, using only wood, no manure. Now, says Virginia Romero, Mrs. Duran "does it the Taos way."

Both women speak with affection of the mica that makes their pots unique. Picuris clay is micaceous, but Virginia Duran gives her pots their sparkle mostly with a slip of mica rubbed on at the end of shaping, before firing. She says, "Around here there are two or three kinds of clay, but only one is good. We are strict with the clay, and with the work, too. The mica comes from a different place, in blocks like gold. Then we soak it and it gets slippery."

Virginia Romero doesn't add anything to her Taos clay: "It's just one clay, it has a little bit mica in it already." She cleans and grinds the raw clay ("I grind the clay fine; that's why I never lose pots in firing."). Then she soaks it overnight until the mica is "tender." When she divides the clay into the ten or fifteen pots she shapes in a day, "sometimes the mica all seems to go in one pot."

Taos pots seem the simplest of Pueblo pottery. Even the firing is simple, since smoke stains (fire clouds) suit the style. Virginia Romero agrees: "I just shape them and smooth them; I don't polish them. I scrape them with a file. I just file them and then I make them smooth with my hand. That's all."

The pots belie her humility. The mica glows as gold as sun-warmed adobe. Picuris pots can be bronze or even reddish orange. Subtle modeling decorates some: a sinuous ribbon of extra clay; a band of small knobs; the soft curves of a lizard bulging out from the pot, seeming almost to come through the surface. The shapes are distinctive, too: tall, round-bottomed vases similar to Apache and Navajo pots, and bean pots with handles and lids.

Not Just For Pretty

Micaceous pots are the last of the purely utilitarian unpainted Pueblo pottery. Virginia Duran says that Tewa and Rio Grande pieces are "just for pretty. A long time ago they made good pottery, but not now." To a Picuris potter, "good" pottery means useful pottery. Mrs. Duran judges Picuris pots "very handy in any way." In northern New Mexico, tradition states flatly that no beans taste better than those cooked in a Picuris bean pot.

The micaceous clay fires waterproof, but local cooks still seal the inside of a bean pot with oil to keep food from tasting too earthy. Virginia Romero says you can set one of her pots right on a stovetop burner: "It's real done so you could use it any way you want." Virginia Duran recommends covering an open flame with a piece of metal to protect the pot from direct heat. The heated pot keeps food hot for hours.

Taos and Picuris people made decorated pottery before the Pueblo Rebellion in 1680, but since then they have made only utilitarian micaceous pottery in the style of the Jicarilla Apaches. Tewa potters have made micaceous pottery as well, but usually by adding a mica slip to their more refined nonmicaceous clay to give the pot the surface glitter of Taos and Picuris pottery. Jicarilla people also make pottery with a rich micaceous finish, signing their pieces "J.A.T." for Jicarilla Apache Tribe.

*Pottery by Cora Durand and her grandson
Anthony on the mantel of her Picuris home.*

Made in Taos

Just what makes a Taos pot? Is it the micaceous clay, or the old style of making it? Does it have to be made by a Taos Indian?

Bernice Suazo-Naranjo provides one answer. The pottery is "an extension of myself and who I am. People from other pueblos and tribes can borrow the clay. There are many potters who are non-Indian who make beautiful micaceous pots. But Taos Pueblo is a unique pueblo. My work becomes unique because I was born and raised in Taos. When people accept my work, they are accepting a lot of me."

Bernice began making pottery in 1981. She had lived away from the pueblo for many years, and in some ways she saw pottery as a way to reenter her traditions. She and her husband Tito both came from "pottery families"—Bernice, from Taos; Tito, from Santa Clara. They had the "outline" of potterymaking in their minds, from gathering clay to firing, but learned the fine points by trial and error. At first, Bernice was overwhelmed by the amount of information her grandmother gave her: "The way grandmothers express themselves, you've got to be there and do it, they are not going to explain, step by step."

Now, after learning from many hundreds of pieces, she makes large micaceous pots free of fire clouds, with her bold, distinctive designs carved into the clay and painted with red slip. She believes in the old way, using pure micaceous clay, and speaks with excitement about probing the frontiers of shaping this coarse, difficult material. "I think the clay calls for simplicity. When I go overboard with a design, it just doesn't satisfy me.

"I want to let other people know pottery is not dead in Taos," she says. "When you see the pot come out of the firing, it's unbelievable the high you get because you know that you've done it yourself. It's something that you just created out of nothing, just the clay, all made by hand. If I and other young Taos potters don't do pottery, pretty soon we will only be seeing pottery in the books."

For potterymaking can indeed die within a pueblo. At Picuris, the primary clay source, on land just outside the pueblo's reservation, has been destroyed by road construction and mining. Older potters like Virginia Duran do not have the energy to search out new clay pits. They simply quit potting.

But pottery is not dead at Picuris. On feast day, Cora Durand and her grandson Anthony have a "Pottery For Sale" sign in the window of their house facing the plaza. A stack of ponderosa pine bark in their yard sits next to a grill, ready for firing bronze-colored bean pots, cookie jars, creamers, and sugar bowls—all with the Picuris trademark twinkle of mica. Cora and another Picuris potter teach a small class for the younger women. Pottery remains one of the few means of support in this isolated valley, and the enterprising young people of Picuris will see to it that the traditions continue.

*Bernice Suazo-Naranjo,
Taos potter.*

CHAPTER THREE

The Red and the Black: Tewa Pueblos

LOIS GUTIERREZ puts four black, terraced symbols on the rims of her Santa Clara bowls to represent the four sacred Tewa mountains. Says her husband, Derek de la Cruz, "Our clays, our paints, all come from within those four original mountains. So we put them on our pottery: San Antonio Peak at the north, Sandia on the south, Tsikomo at the top of the Jemez on the west, and Lake Peak or Truchas Peaks on the east in the Sangre de Cristo."

Between these sacred mountains, within a great bowl created by the barriers of the Jemez and Sangre de Cristo ranges, the Tewa pueblos lie in the Rio Grande badlands between Española and Santa Fe: San Juan and Santa Clara, respectively, just north and south of Española; San Ildefonso, on the Rio Grande where the Los Alamos highway crosses the river; Nambe and Pojoaque, more loosely knit and dispersed among the Hispanic ranches along the base of the Sangre de Cristos; and proudly independent Tesuque, just north of Santa Fe.

These small villages (San Juan is the largest, with some eighteen hundred people) are among the best known pueblos, partly because of their long association with the centers of Anglo and Hispanic colonization in New Mexico, and partly because of their pottery.

Left, *melon jars by the late Helen Shupla, Santa Clara (Richard M. Howard collection);* above, *Mimbres-inspired feather-patterned jar by Maria and Santana Martinez, San Ildefonso (Wheelwright Museum Shop).*

The two northern pueblos, San Juan and Santa Clara, traditionally made polished pottery without designs. In a freely burning oxidizing fire, their pots fired red; a smothered reducing fire yielded black pottery. In former times Tewas traded with Hispanic people from near Canjilon, north of San Juan, for the red clay painted as slip on both red and black pottery. "Tewa red" now comes, ironically, from Santo Domingo. But as Derek would point out, Santo Domingo still falls within the area defined by the four sacred Tewa mountains.

Historically, the other four Tewa pueblos made both undecorated and painted pieces, but these traditions turned topsy-turvy in the early twentieth century when potterymaking became an income-producing profession. The force behind the change was the little pueblo of San Ildefonso, in the center of Tewa country. The drive came mostly from one exceptional woman, Maria Martinez.

Maria

In 1918, only eighty-three people survived an influenza epidemic at San Ildefonso Pueblo, just twenty-five miles north of Santa Fe. Now, it is hard to imagine how isolated the pueblo was in those days. And poor. With much of their land taken by neighboring Hispanic and Anglo people, the fields troubled by drought and too few men to work them, and the tribe's watershed rapidly being logged off, San Ildefonso people were in trouble. The other Tewa pueblos had similar problems.

Two remarkable people, Maria and Julian Martinez, were among the survivors of that epidemic. Maria and Julian had already been making pottery to sell for ten years. They started with polychrome in the style popular with San Ildefonso potters in the late 1800s, made for the tourist market that came with the completion of the railroad to Albuquerque in 1880. Maria shaped and polished the pots; Julian painted them.

Archaeologists under the direction of Edgar Hewett, working in the ruins at nearby Bandelier National Monument, asked Maria to reproduce vessels styled after broken pots they had dug from ancestral Pueblo homes. In doing so, Maria made some of the finest pots yet made in San Ildefonso—thin-walled, hard-fired gray pots decorated by Julian with fine black lines. Then they began to make black pottery fired in manure-smothered blazes, as Santa Clara, San Juan, and San Ildefonso potters had done for many years. With a slightly cooler firing, they sacrificed a bit of hardness but gained a deeper, jet-black finish.

The smoothly polished blackware began to sell well, but that left Julian with nothing to do. His designs, painted in vegetal guaco paint, disappeared from

Maria and Julian Martinez of San Ildefonso, circa 1930s.
(Museum of New Mexico #30466)

the blackware in the firing, so he stopped painting. Then one day in about 1919, he experimented by painting a design on one of Maria's pots after she had polished it, using the clay slip she had used for polishing. Neither of them knew just what would happen in the firing.

What did happen was a new kind of pottery—matte black (where Julian had painted) on polished black (where Maria's carefully rubbed slip still showed). Julian's invention caught on immediately. San Ildefonso black-on-black pottery became so popular that by 1925, several families in the pueblo supported themselves with money from pottery sales.

Julian loved designing. He kept a notebook of ideas he gathered from pots that caught his fancy. He revived ancient designs and transformed them to match his artistic vision: the plumed water serpent with forked lightning for its tongue (called *avanyu* in Tewa) and the old Mimbres radiating feather pattern became his hallmarks. Julian likened the water serpent to the leading edge of a flash flood pushing down an arroyo. When Maria spent their pottery money on a Model-T, Julian even painted the new car with matte-black designs.

Adam and Santana Martinez, San Ildefonso.

Julian's creativity and Maria's skill and determination combined to make Pueblo pottery more than useful: they made it an individualized art and a profession. Julian died in 1943, but Maria continued making pottery until 1972. Her daughter-in-law Santana decorated the pots until 1956, when Maria's son Popovi Da took over. Popovi died in 1971; Maria in 1980. Maria's youngest sister, Clara, was the polishing master in the family throughout these years, and still is today.

The whole family collaborated. Maria always said that what mattered most was that it was San Ildefonso pottery, not that a particular woman made a particular pot. Especially when she was younger, Maria obligingly signed almost any well-made San Ildefonso blackware when asked to—much to the consternation of collectors and dealers concerned with the origin of pots signed with her name.

Maria's legacy remains—the rejuvenation of potterymaking at San Ildefonso and other pueblos and the creation of a livelihood at home, where the old traditions can be nourished. Today, Santana and Adam (Maria's oldest son), at seventy-five and eighty-three years old, still make pottery in the style of Maria and Julian. Their daughters and granddaughters and great-grandsons—plus an assortment of cousins—make pottery. Santana says, "It's good that the children and grandchildren are making pottery, but there is no one to help me paint since Adam's eyes started to go bad." Maria's great-granddaughter Kathy Sanchez explains: "Santana needs someone to stay with her and help her. Her granddaughters, we say we'll come on weekends but then there is so much to do. Not enough time and too many other worries in our heads. Painting is hard. We make the etched pots, the sgraffito, because they are easier—we can fire them and then just put them on the shelf until we have time to decorate."

Barbara Gonzales, another of Santana and Adam's granddaughters, makes incised pots but also has begun making the painted polychrome revived by Popovi Da in the 1950s and 1960s. For sgraffito pots she often works with the two-tone style, also developed by Popovi, in which the pot is fired more than once, successive firings burning off the black to selectively let the red—transformed to sienna—show again. Popovi's son Tony Da crafted spectacular sgrafitto pots until he returned to his first love, painting.

Barbara's willingness to experiment characterizes her family and the younger generation of Pueblo potters in general. She credits Maria with being the "major force behind getting clay recognized as an art form," and calls herself a "clay artist" rather than simply a potter: "As an artist, if you let yourself go you will find yourself doing different things."

Carved water-serpent jar made at San Ildefonso by Rose Gonzales in 1939. (School of American Research collection)

Earth Colors and Carved Serpents

Other pottery families work at San Ildefonso, and Blue Corn claims hers is "the noisiest family in the pueblo." She began making pottery when she was three years old. "My grandmother had persuaded me how to make pottery. She was blind, and she used to feel my hand and feel my face, and she told me I was going to be a potter. So here I am."

Polychrome San Ildefonso plate by Blue Corn. (Katherine H. Rust Children's Collection, Albuquerque, courtesy Mudd-Carr Gallery)

At first, Blue Corn made only black pottery, but one day she and her husband found a sherd from a prehistoric pot—a polychrome pot. She said to him, "Why don't we try and do this?"

First they had to find the right clay. Says Blue Corn, "I walked, I walked, I walked, and finally I found some clay—different color of clay." Her first experiments came out lavender and bright green. " 'Oh my gosh, what am I doing here?' I said to myself, 'Gee, these colors don't look right to me.' "

She kept experimenting, going to Black Mesa for white slip, up towards Los Alamos for clays that yielded gold, pink, and dark red; avocado, rust, and beige. "All of my pots has that earth color." She learned to polish the new slip: "It's very hard to do, but still we just went ahead and did that."

Blue Corn sums up the way she feels about pottery: "I don't work to bring a lot of award to my pueblo, or to my house. I just like to make pottery, that's all. Sometimes when my pottery cracks in the firing I feel like quitting, but it's the only thing I know. I said if I quit I will never start all over again. Then I'm going to make the kids feel bad. They'll say that my mom is not making any more pottery and maybe I better not make any more. And I think if they carry on the potterymaking, that they have a lot of hope."

Rose Gonzales was another innovator at San Ildefonso. She came to the pueblo from San Juan when she married a San Ildefonso man in 1920 and learned potterymaking from her mother-in-law. In the 1930s, Rose made the first modern carved pottery at the pueblo. While out deer hunting, her husband found a potsherd decorated by carving, and as she says, "I just started from there." Rose carves her pottery with distinctive rounded edges. Her black and red polished and carved pots now span some fifty years.

Rose Gonzales taught her art to her son Tse-Pe and his wife Dora. First with Tse-Pe and now on her own, Dora Tse Pe Peña carries on Rose's traditions. "I love her work and I love carving. And I love the water serpent. It depicts water—rain, thanksgiving, and prayer for water. It's a San Ildefonso trademark. I like to make my serpent really simple and graceful. You'll notice that Santa Clara serpents look almost oriental, all the curves on the backs and all. Mine are very plain."

Dora, who grew up at Zia, the daughter of potter Candelaria Gachupin, also married into San Ildefonso. She made a few pots with her mother, and after she married, a few with Rose Gonzales. Now she has been able to teach her own daughters potterymaking. "I tell them, make one good pot instead of ten bad pots." Dora makes old-style carved black, red, and unslipped pottery, but also makes black-and-sienna pots, sometimes adding micaceous slips and, after firing, turquoise inlay and sgraffito. "If I add anything from Zia, it's just shapes, like the water jar shape."

She says, "There are some pots that I become especially attached to and I wish I could keep them. When I sell a pot and pack it and I'm giving it to a person, I say words to it, from my heart. I say, well I'll see you again sometime. If today were a hundred years ago, the pot wouldn't be going anywhere, it would be at the kiva. It would be sacred and I would see it often and I would feel like there is a part of me here. And I feel that way about the pots that go away now. I feel like something special in my life is going to Florida or California—or wherever it goes."

Russell Sanchez also learned a lot from watching his great-aunt Rose Gonzales, and Dora, too. The most active of the youngest generation of San Ildefonso potters, he includes in his work two-tone black and sienna jars with bear-effigy lids, inlaid stones, and green slips. Russell says, "I feel my work is very traditional but because of the designs they are called nontraditional. People forget that ceremonial pots have had stones set in them for a long time. And colors fascinate me. The green slip comes from up north in Colorado, and near Abiquiu. You can use traditional techniques and materials and still come up with something far-out and a little different. You really can't define tradition."

Carved water-serpent bowl by Teresita Naranjo, Santa Clara. (School of American Research collection)

The Home of the Black

Santa Claras speak wistfully whenever San Ildefonso blackware comes up in conversation. They respect Maria Martinez for her revitalization of Pueblo pottery and acknowledge the other fine San Ildefonso potters for their craft. But it hurts them when people forget that Maria and Julian invented matte-black decoration, not blackware itself. San Ildefonso and Santa Clara potters had long made blackware, and Santa Clara has been its stronghold for three centuries.

Mary Cain says, "My grandmother has been doing it, and her mother, and she learned from my grandmother's great-grandmother—all in a line, the black pottery, all through their lives." Black vessels, particularly large storage jars with an indented bear paw design, are emblematic of Santa Clara pottery. For years, Mary Cain's aunt Margaret Tafoya has made one huge black storage jar each year, along with many smaller pieces. Several dozen Santa Clara potters in the Tafoya and Naranjo families trace themselves to the same grandparents that Mary Cain talks about—Sarafina and Geronimo Tafoya.

Many legends tell the story of the bear paw; one says that a bear led the Santa Claras to water during a drought, and in remembrance of this act of salvation, Santa Clara potters began placing its tracks on their work. Another distinctive Santa Clara shape is the double-spouted, strap-handled wedding jar. Many pueblos make this form, and until recently, Santa Clara people continued to use them in their weddings, as well.

Rose Naranjo says, "I like to make wedding vases. It reminds me of how one of my uncles was getting married and my grandmother took a wedding vase and it was passed around to all family that was there and they drank out of it—the men's relatives on one spout, the women's folk on the other spout.

And then they make a holy water and when they finish that, they just break it into many pieces. They say the marriage would last. I don't know how it would last in many broken pieces; that I couldn't understand."

Belen Tapia adds, "Now they hate to break it. If they use it they just put flowers in it today, on the table. It's very hard to make wedding vases. Polishing them and the animals are hardest. When they don't come out good we have to sandpaper them and do it over again. When we are getting ready for the annual Indian Market in Santa Fe, sometimes I have to sandpaper plates six or seven times."

Val and Pula Gutierrez agree about the challenges of polishing. Their blackware animals—bears, beavers, turtles, pigs, horses, penguins, ducks, and skunks—are fragile enough that an arm or leg may break during polishing. A big bear, shaped by Val and polished by Pula, takes a full day to polish. When tourists ask if they use a machine for polishing, Val points to Pula and says "there's our machine."

Mary Cain, Santa Clara potter, with a finished jar and an unpainted, unpolished wedding vase.

A Santa Clara storage jar made by Margaret Tafoya, decorated with the bearpaw impression. (Rick Dillingham collection)

Belen Tapia calls the bearpaw and the melon bowl "the old folks' designs." When she makes melon jars, which have an even pattern of sculptured squash ribs around them, she starts with an extra thick bowl and cuts the grooves when the clay is still soft. After drying and sanding, polishing inside the grooves takes extra time. The late Helen Shupla was proud that the ribs of her melon bowls stretched nearly all the way from the rim to the base; in her bowls, the grooves could be felt both inside and outside the pots.

Deeper carving is another characteristic Santa Clara style, mostly in black pottery, but in redware, too. The carver cuts away the background, leaving the design standing in relief. The design and body are polished, and the background is matte painted.

When the pottery is leather hard, the carver goes to work. Stella Chavarria uses woodcarving tools, screwdrivers, and one kitchen paring knife sharpened so many times that its blade sticks out only an inch or so from the hilt—her favorite tool. She says, "I draw it out in pencil first. Everybody says that it looks easy for me to carve, but I guess after doing it for so many years you don't really think about it, you just do it.

"You have to be careful as to how far along you want them to dry, then put them in a plastic bag. I'm very forgetful, and sometimes one dries a little bit too much. Then it's hard on your hands and it chips a lot. But when they are just right, carving is my favorite part. I could sit here forever carving and let somebody else do the rest. The only thing is, when it's real quiet it gives you too much time to think."

Beyond the Red and the Black

Santa Clara potters have become famous as innovators. In the 1930s, Lela and Van Gutierrez modified a polychrome method already in their family. The resulting style is so distinctive that pottery by the Gutierrez family is uniquely their own. Margaret and Luther Gutierrez have carried on the work of their parents, and with Luther's granddaughter Stephanie now potting, the style already spans four generations. On a tan background above a red base, they paint intricate designs in a wide spectrum of pastel colors. The Gutierrezes polish with a rag instead of a stone, giving their pots and whimsical animal figures a silky feel rather than the mirrorlike brilliance of stone polish. They keep their clay sources secret.

Belen and Ernest Tapia work in the "traditional" polychrome style of Santa Clara. They make polished redware painted with white, buff, blue-gray, and matte red. Ernest Tapia says, "She makes the pottery, but I do all the designing. I seen those old folks' pottery. You take some of their design, then put

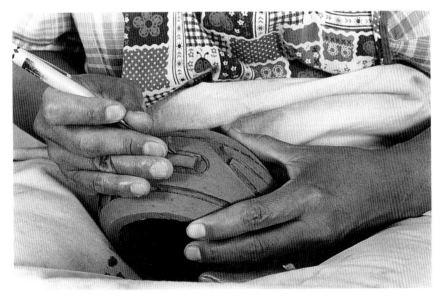

Stella Chavarria carving Santa Clara pottery.

them together with some design of your own, and before you know it you've got something different—and better. San Ildefonso's got their own, and here we've got our own, too. San Juan's got their own. People may say, well it's just all pottery. But it's really not. It's the art that they put in; it's got to have a meaning."

Petra Gutierrez belongs to another "polychrome family." Her daughters are half Santa Clara and half Pojoaque. Minnie Vigil and Lois Gutierrez live at Santa Clara, Thelma Talachy and daughter-in-law Virginia Gutierrez at Pojoaque. Another daughter, Goldenrod Garcia, does sgrafitto pots.

Lois began making pottery with her husband, Derek de la Cruz, as her partner. Today she signs her pottery alone. Lois and Derek have developed a distinctive slip by adding white to dark-gold clay to make a buff background color. Lois takes lizards, hummingbirds, and humpbacked flute players and expands them into designs that encircle her large jars like murals.

Derek walks the hills in search of new clays. Lois says that he nearly always "sticks in an experiment whenever we're firing to see how a certain color is going to come out." Derek says, "If you listen closely enough and pay attention to the earth, it really does speak. It tells you what's what. And you learn from it. But you've got to go out there and listen. It's taken us fifteen years to learn how to mix all our colors."

The hotter the fire, the better the colors. Lois and Derek have learned that the pots come out gray if the fire isn't hot enough, but a second firing will burn off the smoke clouds and bring up the colors. Lois says, "My favorite part is firing. When it fires good, you know that your time and your work has been worth it. There's nothing nicer than firing when it's really cold out, and you're standing there drinking a hot cup of coffee and watching the fire. It gives us a little time to ourselves, too, when we are out of the house. I think the best part, though, is taking it down and finding that it fired good."

Another branch of the huge Tafoya family popularized the sgraffito style in the 1970s. Inspired by the work of Popovi and Tony Da, Grace Medicine Flower and her brother Joseph Lonewolf make mostly miniatures in black and red. Some of their techniques remain family secrets, but to create two-tone pots, a portion of a piece sometimes is covered during firing to keep it from turning black, a method called resist firing. Grace says, "When we realized that the younger kids were making two-color pots by burning off the color after firing with an acetylene torch, we thought it wasn't worth it for us to lose so many pots in firing. So now we make just the one color, black or red." Their designs are precisely incised: Mimbres animals (Grace's favorites are butterflies and hummingbirds) and scenes from Tewa mythology and life.

Lois Gutierrez-de la Cruz and her polychrome Santa Clara pottery.

Another Tafoya cousin, Nancy Youngblood-Cutler, makes miniatures in old-style black—tiny, swirling melon bowls, for example, intricately carved in perfect proportion to full-sized pieces. Her aunt, Mary Archuleta, watches Nancy and her brother Nathan make miniatures, and knows that little pots take just as much time as large ones. Mary says, "I just want to build big ones. Some have the fingers to make small ones. Everything—all their tools—is miniature, right down to the polishing stones. Whatever you're good at, that's what you do."

Rose Naranjo's daughter Jody Folwell has created still another style. She makes her pots in the old way, but often sculpts them in asymmetrical shapes and unusual colors, "not too far from the traditional pots but enough so that I could start a different direction." At times, her incised designs are reminiscent of prehistoric painted designs. Other times, they tell a contemporary story. "I do not think of them really as pottery, I think of them as a piece of artwork that has something to say, statements in life. I think of myself as being a contemporary potter and a traditionalist at the same time. Combining the two is emotional and exciting."

Jody's sister, Nora Naranjo-Morse, makes elegantly abstract figures. Jody reintroduced her to clay when Nora came home to the pueblo in her twenties. "Holding that clay was the first time I ever felt a connection with something greater than myself. I became addicted immediately. I had come home."

As the youngest daughter, Nora says she always wanted to be different. "So I began making animals and people rather than bowls. They tell stories. They always had quirks, character, that defined them as strange. One night I was working on a woman. I wanted her to be in motion but she couldn't because she was clay. Then I shifted her weight onto one leg and twisted her. And I had a rush of adrenaline when that worked that was too important for me as a human being to disregard."

Every day, Nora has "six precious hours" to work in her studio while her kids are at school. "I enter a different frame of mind in there. I'm not afraid to add something like telephone wire to one of my clay people because this clay is with me now in the twentieth century. All the things that affect me— an American Indian woman making pottery now in 1986—come out in my work. Pottery is for everybody; it goes beyond just Pueblo women making pottery and feeling good.

"It makes sense that whatever emotion I bring in to the studio is released into the clay. You're touching it. It's a circle, the connection between me and the finished product. People that react to my pieces enter the circle. They are involved in the experience. That's what pottery is all about for me."

Nora Naranjo-Morse of Santa Clara and one of her "clay people," a koshare *clown figurine.*

New and Old Traditions

San Juan Pueblo, north of Santa Clara, has its own traditions. Like the pottery made at Santa Clara, the old San Juan pottery was mostly undecorated red and black. Their typical jars were two-tone, polished red above unslipped tan, or black above gray when baked in a smothered fire. This banded effect can still be seen in the two most common modern styles.

"Modern" is a tricky word. The new style is really a very old style. In the 1930s, a group of San Juan potters led by Regina Cata sifted through the ancestral sherds and chose Potsuwi'i Incised, made from 1450 to 1500, for a "new" San Juan pottery style. They combined simple patterns of incised lines in unslipped tan on the middle band with a highly polished red rim and base. Micaceous slip, painted in the carved lines, gave them a familiar glitter. Several potters still work in this style, including Rosita de Herrera.

Mary E. Archuleta, who was raised at Santa Clara but who married into San Juan, makes both Santa Clara- and San Juan-style pottery. In some pieces, she combines the two, carving her incised lines extra deep to hold the mica, or polishing San Juan-tan feathers on one side of a red Santa Clara water serpent jar. Mary says the old San Juan bowls with plain polished red above unslipped unpolished tan are "quite tricky. You just have to know where to put the polishing stone on so it won't stick. You just have to *know*."

Another banded San Juan style fills the unpolished middle ground between the reds with polychrome designs, sometimes with the colors outlined by incising or carving. Carnation and Bill Lockwood work in this style, though Bill says, "It's work but it's not real work; we have a real good time with it, and I think it shows in the pieces. It takes a combination of mood, knowledge, and patience."

San Juan pots by Rosita de Herrera. (Ortega's Turquoise Mesa)

Carnation makes bowls up to ten inches high without coiling—from a single ball of clay. She and her sister began making pottery after their mother died. They cleaned out her storage shed, found her tools, and said, "Let's make some pottery." Her son Bill sometimes incises designs on the rims of her polychrome pieces. Though he took his materials with him when he went to college in Albuquerque, he couldn't work there. "There's something about being home," he says.

Home for Virginia Gutierrez is Pojoaque Pueblo, but she was raised in Nambe. Her aunt was the last working Nambe potter in mid-century, and Virginia learned from her. Influenced by her husband's family, the Gutierrezes of Santa Clara, she has developed her own polychrome style: "To me the design is part Nambe and part my own."

"I started with black pottery," says Virginia. "There were so many people making black pottery like Santa Clara, and Nambe wasn't originally known for black pottery. We're known mostly for the micaceous cooking pots, although they have in the past made pottery with designs. So I started into this polychrome and I've had real good luck with it."

Her designs are complex. "I just sit there and think what would look nice on a piece of pottery. Sometimes I do them on paper or I just use the same design over again. Or put all different kinds of designs together and put it on the pot. The sun design is my favorite."

Her clays come from both Nambe and Pojoaque, her sand from Nambe, her clay paints from all over northern New Mexico. "Wherever we go I always take my little baggies with me and I ask my husband to stop when I see a different shade of clay in the hills. I try the sample out and the ones that I like or that work well with my clay I continue to use."

Virginia Gutierrez does not polish her pottery, so she must take extra time with sanding and smoothing to make sure her paint will go on easily. Her shapes include seed jars, completely closed except for a tiny opening: "If you mix your clay the right texture, why you can do just about anything, any form. You can never duplicate your pottery; you try to make one the same, but I've never been able to."

At Tesuque, some black-on-white pottery is still made, along with pieces that are brightly painted after firing, nativity sets, and figurines called "rain gods." Lorencita Pino sculpts spectacular human faces on the sides of her micaceous ware. Manuel Vigil, with his wife, Vicenta, makes exuberant nativities and storytellers complete with woven clothing and rabbit-fur hair.

Though galleries do not boast shelves full of Tesuque pottery, that could change at any time. A Tesuque woman or man, having lived elsewhere, may come home intent on staying in the village and start potting to make that possible. One potter from among the more than two hundred at Santa Clara may marry into Tesuque: the blast of energy from a single determined artist could meld with the old traditions in a new way.

Potterymaking traditions are strong, even when they are invisible. They can die away to a memory—to nothing more than broken sherds and a few pots in museum collections—and then come back to life through the art of a single potter. As Dora Tse Pe Peña says, "I didn't know that I could do pottery. I didn't plan to make my living this way. It was just in me. It's a gift, and I'm grateful for it."

Seed jars and plates by Virginia Gutierrez of Pojoaque–Nambe. (Packard's)

CHAPTER FOUR

Storytellers and Birds:
Middle Rio Grande Pueblos

I N NEW MEXICO, La Bajada Hill divides the Pueblo world in two. Here, some fifteen miles south of Santa Fe, the rim of the high desert plateau that connects the Sangre de Cristo and Jemez mountains drops fifteen hundred feet to the lower deserts. Rio Arriba, the upper river, gives way to Rio Abajo, the lower river.

North of La Bajada lies Tewa country and the mountain villages of Taos and Picuris. Southward, pueblos where Keresan is spoken line the river, first Cochiti at the foot of La Bajada Hill, then Santo Domingo and San Felipe. The people of Cochiti and Santo Domingo think of Santa Fe, to the north, as "town," and both pueblos have been strongly influenced by Tewa potters. Their use of vegetal guaco paint, for example, was learned from the Tewas. Pueblos to the south and west all traditionally use mineral-based black, using only beeweed for binder, if anything. In turn, "Tewa red," the slip that makes both red and black Tewa pottery, comes from Santo Domingo—the same clay that some Santo Domingos use as red paint in their polychrome.

Left, *Mary Trujillo and her Cochiti drummer;* above, *Zia bird on a water jar by Eusebia Shije (Richard M. Howard collection).*

Sandia and Isleta, where the language is Tiwa, flank Albuquerque on its north and south. And in the red mesas sweeping around the southern Jemez Mountains, tucked in along the Jemez River at the brink of the Colorado Plateau, lie Jemez (where the only people who speak Towa live), Zia, and Santa Ana pueblos.

The Rio Abajo begins with Cochiti on the west bank of the Rio Grande. The rough mesas and cliffs of the Pajarito Plateau rise above it, sheltering ruins, the pueblo's ancestral homes, today preserved in Bandelier National Monument. Cochiti people have been generous in sharing their stories, and from them comes the best-known tale of the first Pueblo potters.

Long ago, Clay Old Woman and Clay Old Man came to visit the Cochitis. Clay Old Woman mixed clay with sand and began to coil a pot while Clay Old Man danced beside her. All the people watched. When the pot was some eighteen inches high, Clay Old Man danced too close and kicked it over. He took the broken pot, rolled the clay in a ball, and gave a piece to all the women in the village, telling them never to forget to make pottery. Ever since, when the Cochitis do not make pottery, Clay Old Woman and Clay Old Man come to the village and dance to remind the people of their gift of clay.

From Stories to Storytellers

It is not an easy gift. Mary Trujillo says, "When you do Cochiti pottery, the art is in knowing how to put the slip on and in the firing. You have to have patience."

The white slip on Cochiti dough bowls acquires a patina over the years. Bowls encountered today are likely to have developed such a finish, for few modern Cochiti potters make the traditional bowls painted with black and red flowers, animals, clouds, lightning, and geometric designs, all on an open ground of white slip. Most Cochitis now create figurines.

Figurative pottery comes from an old tradition. Prehistoric Pueblo potters made human-effigy vessels, fired and unfired human and animal figurines, duck canteens, and animal pitchers. Historic Cochiti potters shaped bird pots with beaks as spouts and painted a multitude of animal forms on pots. Many were condemned as "idols" and destroyed by the Spaniards. Others were dismissed as toys and curiosities. But with the coming of the railroad to New Mexico in 1880 and a ready market for their work, Cochiti potters expanded their array of figurines into whole villages of human figures, including cowboys, tourist caricatures, priests, circus performers and dancing bears, and the "singing mother"—a woman holding a child.

Cochiti storytellers by (left) Rita Lewis, (center) Helen Cordero, and (right) Ada Suina. (Wheelwright Museum Shop)

A century later, the figurine tradition is stronger than ever, with the Cochitis inventing new forms every year. The most famous figurine is the "storyteller." Most people use the word loosely today, but storytellers have been made only since 1964, when Helen Cordero created them.

At that time, Helen had been making pottery for only a few years. She had asked her husband's cousin Juanita Arquero to teach her, which not only started Helen but also encouraged Juanita to make pottery again for the first time since she had been a girl. Juanita made bowls, but Helen's bowls always "came out crooked." Juanita suggested she try figures, and for Helen, "it was like a flower blooming." She made singing mothers and nativities, the latter including cows marked with the Cochiti brand.

When folk-art collector Alexander Girard (creator of the remarkable Girard Wing of the Museum of International Folk Art in Santa Fe) bought one of Helen's singing mothers, he asked her to make a larger figure with children.

Helen went home and "kept seeing my grandfather. That one, he was a really good storyteller and there were always lots of us grandchildrens around him."

Her first storyteller, sold to Girard in 1964, had five children hanging from the seated grandfather. As many as thirty children perch on her later pieces. Her style is distinctive: "His eyes are closed because he's thinking; his mouth is open because he's singing." Many other Helen Cordero figures followed the storyteller—a drummer; Navajo storytellers; a turtle "taking children for a ride to learn the old ways"; the "Children's Hour," with older kids grouped around the storyteller.

Many other Cochiti potters followed Helen Cordero's lead. Of the more than two hundred Pueblo potters now making figurative pottery, one-fourth are Cochiti. More than in any other form of pottery, figurative potters can mix their personality with their clay. They can create scenes from daily life, tell stories with humor, and paint the faces of their favorite people. Seferina Ortiz makes lizard, frog, and owl storytellers; Martha Arquero makes kangaroo storytellers; Mary Frances Herrera shapes miniatures, storytellers starting at three-quarters of an inch; and Tony Dallas and Tim Cordero (part Hopi) make mudhead clown storytellers. The possibilities are as varied as the personal histories of the potters.

Mary Trujillo, daughter of Leonidas Tapia, one of the great San Juan potters, is married to Helen Cordero's adopted son. Mary worked for many years as a counselor at the Institute of American Indian Arts in Santa Fe, and when she moved to Cochiti in 1978, Ada Suina taught her to make storytellers.

Mary also takes her inspiration for faces from her grandfather. She hangs a drawing of him prominently on her wall: "When I do storytellers with braids like him, there really is something special about it." She says her first storyteller "looked like Heckel and Jeckel." But from the beginning, they sold, "and that encourages you.

"Everything that I do, I pray that it comes out right. I pray to my mother, I pray to Maria, to help me have their gift." Working with the delicate white slip, Mary needs their blessing. The figures can be modeled from white or red clay, but if red clay is used, it takes ten to fifteen coats of white to cover it. The slip goes on after the pot has been warmed in the oven. With each layer, the potter uses a clean, white rag to polish off the chalky film, then back in the oven it goes.

Mary's teacher, Ada Suina, says it takes "coats and coats" to properly slip the pieces. "I never even count." One piece takes a half day of sitting in front of her kitchen stove, set at 350 degrees. Earlier potters used woodstoves, and in the old days, Ada says that Cochitis slipped their pottery only in summer, using a washtub to create a makeshift oven heated by the New Mexico sun.

Animal figurine by Damacia Cordero of Cochiti. (Wheelwright Museum Shop)

Mermaids and Angels, Dinosaurs and Bears

Says Ada Suina, "Once you start a phase or style, it seems to stay the same. I can't change my faces—they just come."

Ivan and Rita Lewis agree. "We just start building and then decide. You start it and something comes out." Both are from pottery families: Rita is from Cochiti, and Ivan is the son of Acoma potter Lucy Lewis. At first Ivan helped Rita part time, but she kept saying to him, "All your sisters and brothers are potters; you ought to be." When he retired, he began making his own pieces. Now, he makes the larger (16–18 inch) storytellers and dough bowls, while Rita makes their smaller pieces: storytellers, angels, and nativities. Ivan does most of the sanding, and Rita does the fine painting.

Ivan has also revived some of the historic figurines of the railroad era—cowboys and caricatures. "The old ones just give you an idea, you can't really copy. It always develops and comes out your own way." He also makes mermaids. "Cochiti mermaids? Sure, they live up in Cochiti Lake!"

Ivan and Rita work together. Ivan says, "We talk to them. We're always joking around. Sometimes we laugh as they are taking shape—this one's coming out crooked, this one has a big belly. I tell Rita that I can fix anything in the sanding."

Louis Naranjo also has made modern versions of the historic tourist caricatures and his own mermaids. He gets his ideas for caricatures on trips to Santa Fe, "seeing a little boy with his baseball cap to one side eating an ice cream

Ivan Lewis of Cochiti and pottery made with his wife, Rita.

cone, bikini ladies, a girl with a camera." He made an old padre ("a regular priest like you see in the history books") and that gave him the idea for an Indian wedding set. One of his weddings included a pregnant bride and a chagrined groom.

Louis's wife Virginia works with him. Besides storytellers, she makes snakes, kangaroos, giraffes, and dinosaurs. (Damacia Cordero's dinosaurs are also well known.) Virginia "fired some elephants recently, and they fired gray—just like real elephants."

Louis is best known for his bear storytellers. "I thought of the idea when I was hunting deer in the mountains. I saw a bear down in the valley with two cubs climbing all over her. I started my bear figures after that with one cub. Now I'm up to twenty." Louis paints his bears black. Virginia says, "The more you rub your bear, the blacker and shinier it gets."

Louis says, "I love my bears, I really do. They're just like my grandkids to me. You have to put all your heart to it. First, I make the head; that tells me how

Louis Naranjo of Cochiti and his bear storyteller.

big the body will be. From there you can build it up. To put on the little bears, I put a hole through the arm and put a little cone of clay on the bottom of the little bear to attach it."

Other clay persons and animals come from the Naranjo household: antelope and deer dancers; jackalopes (the legendary western jackrabbit with antlers); turtles; an Indian Santa Claus; a drum with bears and drummers hanging from it (Louis got the idea from powwow drum groups); a coyote with little coyotes lined up on its back (Virginia says, "It's the mama giving howling lessons").

Cochiti Dam brought difficulties—as well as mermaids—to the village's potters. The massive construction project destroyed their primary sources of gray clay and white slip. They now use mostly red clay, which requires many more layers of slip to be covered, and white slip comes from a single dwindling supply at Santo Domingo.

But the Cochitis' production hardly reflects these constraints. Their energy and humor seem boundless, and the clay people respond in kind. Mary Trujillo says, "I talk or look at my drummer every day. I tell friends, 'Listen to him and he'll sing for you.'" Adds Helen Cordero, "They come from my heart, and they're singing. Can't you hear them?"

A Santo Domingo storage jar by Robert Tenorio, decorated in a negative-painted style, with a line break through the design. (Wheelwright Museum Shop)

Santo Domingo the Bold

Just a few miles south of Cochiti lies Santo Domingo, with its two active pottery-producing families, the Melchors and the Tenorios. "Conservative" is the word that comes up first in any mention of this pueblo. Their designs are often described as "simple geometrics." These abstractions may be simple, but they are bold.

Frank Harlow and other pottery historians point out that Santo Domingo conservatism is easily seen in the longevity of the pueblo's pottery styles. Some designs popular today have changed little since the 1700s. Even the more recent styles are subtle variations on formal traditions. One such design covers the pot in panels of such big, bold swatches of black and red that only a few lines of the cream-slipped pot show through, a "negative painting" style. Other Santo Domingo pots are freer, with birds and flowers, but rarely with mammals, and never with humans. Unlike neighboring Cochiti, Santo

Domingo religious leaders forbid representations of human figures and a variety of other sacred designs on pottery made for sale.

Santo Domingo birds are distinctive. Robert Tenorio says, "The Santo Domingo bird is usually in a still life, with maybe the tails painted with designs, or the breast area. Whereas the Zia one is usually in action, in flight or jumping. And at Zia, their bodies are more likely solid colors rather than designed."

Santo Domingo pots continue to be used. On feast days, women crisscross the village carrying steaming bowls of food to the kivas. Even the pottery for sale has an air of usefulness—stew bowls and dough bowls, full-sized water jars, and solid-looking storage jars. Says Robert Tenorio, "Most of my bowls are down at home and are still being used in the village. Just to see my things being used—there goes a Tenorio pot or bowl—it's really great. It's something that will be around for a long time, just like all the prehistoric potteries."

Firing was the hardest traditional technique for him to learn. His first Indian Market piece was so black that Robert says a new category had to be created for it: "primitive or historic." "I wasn't competing with anybody," he recalls, "and I won a blue ribbon."

Since then he has refined his firing techniques. "I'm to a point now where I know how to control the heat. The only opening I leave is from the top where I will peek in to see what's happening. It's when it's red hot down there that you know it's done. And then when it cools back down you will see the nice white and the black in there."

Robert's main concern is finding enough white slip. "It's the only thing that turns our spinach juice black. The last time we went we only got half a bucketful. It was a whole day's work because we had to dig with our hands. And just tiny pieces—when we found a good one-inch size, that's a gold nugget for us. We get all excited."

"We checked about twenty places to see if we can find another area. There is an area, it has the same feel as the white, but when it fires it turns yellowish or red instead of white. We're at a point where we may talk to a geologist, but at the same time, I hate to find out what it is because once I know I could go to one of the ceramic places and go buy me kaolin or one of those kinds of glazes. It might be one of them. But though I started that style of designing onto stoneware products, commercial materials—it wasn't the thing for me."

South of Santo Domingo along the slow-moving Rio Grande, San Felipe people make very few painted vessels. No decorated pottery has been made at Sandia Pueblo in historic times. Occasional pottery classes at these two pueblos may inspire a young artist, but that has yet to happen.

Eudora Montoya and her Santa Ana pots.

Lying between them, Santa Ana has a long pottery tradition, but few active potters. The old pueblo itself lies deserted on the Jemez River; Santa Anas live near their farms on the Rio Grande just north of Bernalillo. Here, Eudora Montoya has singlehandedly kept Santa Ana pottery alive for many years.

Eudora and her sisters, whom she has survived by fifty years, began making pottery when their mother died. Her bowls and water jars maintain the old Santa Ana ways: a temper of river sand, historic designs, black paint, and considerable use of red on a chalky-white slip. She collects her gray and red clay and fine sand from Santa Ana land and buys her white slip from Zia.

Eudora's husband has gone blind and no longer works. She says, "I work hard, because he can't see." Large pots are hardest. Sometimes they crack. "To make it good," a big water jar may take three days to design. "I like to smell those water jars when you put the water in and pour it out. The jar smells good. Like rainwater."

She uses the old designs: clouds, and a hooked arc surrounding a circle she calls "turkey eyes." "When I look at the clouds in the sky, it seems to me there's a design on them," she says. Eudora makes bean pots that she leaves a plain red and shapes figures, too—horses, "little ones," and "a drum man with three singers." Her two granddaughters help her, particularly with the small pieces. Recently she has taught her craft to other women in the village. Several have continued making pottery, including Clara Paquin, and a small Santa Ana arts and crafts cooperative exists.

Elizabeth Medina, Zia potter.

Prayers in Pots

Basalt dominates both the village of Zia and its pottery. Zia Pueblo sits on a basalt-capped mesa on the north bank of the Jemez River, commanding a fine view southeast to the Sandia Mountains. North looms the blue summit of the Jemez Mountains. A bridge did not reach the village until 1939, and in his recent study of Zia pottery, Michael Hering realized that 1939 also marked the change from full-scale utilitarian water jars and serving bowls to smaller pottery made strictly for sale.

Zia pots are the only modern Pueblo pots tempered with basalt. Elizabeth Medina says the key to working with the hard volcanic rock is to use as much temper as possible when you mix the clay, more than half of the mixture. That way your pots will not pop in firing. Elizabeth sometimes buries basalt in sand for a full year to soften it before grinding.

"I think Zia potteries are the hardest pots," says Zia potter Eusebia Shije. "Rocks take all your strength. You have to crush it, step by step. I use the grinding stone—coarse, medium, on down."

When Eusebia first began making pottery, she didn't use enough rock, and her pots kept "popping just like a popcorn" in firings. Finally, she mastered the clay, but then "the white slip was a problem. My mom was always on the white and I wanted to do that." Finally, she learned how to carefully apply the white slip, too. Now she says, "I'm always with the clay. That's my income."

Zia potters have been famous for centuries. The Zias had fine pottery but poor agricultural land, a situation reversed at pueblos like Jemez and San Felipe and one that invited trade: food for pots. This system worked with remarkably few people. Michael Hering calculated that in the late nineteenth century, one of the most creatively impressive times at Zia, no more than twenty-five women could have been making pottery in the village.

Zia pottery is stone polished and painted with black pigment (with no bee-weed binder) made exclusively from manganese-rich iron concretions that weather from the sandstone cliffs. Zia potters have used the same red, white, and black pigments since the seventeenth century. The Zia bird is their design hallmark, but it is less widely known that the New Mexico state symbol, a styl-ized sun, comes from an old Zia ceremonial pot.

Zia designs have long been painted on a white-slipped upperbody over a red underbody. The potters say that the red represents the earth and that which is "below or before" the present earth. The designs on the white slip above rep-resent what comes from the earth or what takes place in this world.

Designs include abstract feathers and feathered prayer sticks, birds, vege-tation, clouds, spiderwebs (to catch moisture), lightning, the red arc of a rain-bow, and the curves of drumsticks that make the sound of thunder. Zia pot-ters identify their bird as a roadrunner, sacred symbol of speed, bearer of prayers.

In making an everyday jar to hold water and nourishing foods, the potter creates a prayer for rain—a prayer manifested in clay. The previous third world of existence forms the red base, the white fourth world where we live now forms the upperbody. Each of the design elements resonates with the sym-bolism of rain and new life, and the pivotal spot is held by the bird messenger, swiftly carrying to the skies the people's prayer for rain. A rainbow arcs across the pot, unifying its design and fulfilling its prayers.

Marcellus Medina says, "We still have to maintain our culture in this way. But we can't live in the past. In order for an artist to succeed in this modern world you have to change with the times. One side pulls each way. We can't choose. We live in both worlds."

Marcellus's wife, Elizabeth, makes Zia pottery painted with traditional designs on a beige slip, the family trademark. Carrying on a style created by his parents, Sofia and Rafael Medina, in the 1960s, Marcellus also works with Elizabeth in a unique contemporary style. He uses her fired, unpainted tra-ditional pots as a ground for highly detailed acrylic paintings of Indian dancers with white and black backgrounds. Marcellus's paintings look much like framed works of art, only they have been painted on hand-coiled, ground-fired clay.

"This is my way of showing that it is all right to change," he says. "It is good to change. These are the pots of the future."

He may be right. The Medinas are the most active young potters at Zia. Candelaria Gachupin and Sofia Medina are making fewer pieces than they once did. Eusebia Shije and Helen Gachupin, though master potters, have become discouraged by pitting problems that have worsened in the 1980s. The potters believe the tempering rock is to blame, but Zia clay can contain limestone inclusions that expand months after firing and spall off, leaving a surface pit. Spalling can be found on Zia pottery dating back to 1700—no consolation to Eusebia, who has "tried so many years to try to make a good pot; I don't want people to come back and say, 'Mrs. Shije, you didn't make a good pot.'"

She says, "I really love making potteries, but when something goes wrong when I need money for my children, it's just depressing. I had a whole box of potteries that pitted, and I'll resoak those for a bowl for my own use. I take my time to be a good potter, why should I have to quit? I hate to let my skill go."

The traditions of Zia pottery rest today in a very small number of artists. With the power of their prayers in the pots, the speed of the roadrunners, and centuries of continuity with their past, Zia potters surely will find a way around their problems.

Jemez pot by Juanita Fragua's daughter, Glendora Daubs, decorated with shallowly incised sgraffito-style carving. (Wheelwright Museum Shop)

Jemez: The Problems and Privileges of Freedom

Jemez Pueblo abandoned its traditional styles at the time of the Pueblo Rebellion, a period of dislocation and turmoil. They had painted fine-line, black-on-white designs on their pottery for centuries, but no one has made such pots at the pueblo since 1700.

For years, they traded with Zia—crops from their fertile fields in the Jemez Valley for most of the decorated pottery they needed, making their own plain cooking vessels. With the creation of a commercial market for pottery in the twentieth century, the Jemez people had no living tradition to draw on. Individual potters have tried a multitude of styles since then. One woman used melted pine pitch to make her designs resemble the glaze paints that had been used centuries ago. Another used guaco paint on unslipped pots. Others made pottery in the traditional way, but after firing, painted it with poster paint or acrylics. Such experiments come from not knowing what other pueblos call "the right way," but the lack of community tradition also frees any creative Jemez potter to develop her own style.

Juanita Fragua says, "If I see an old pot, I hate to copy the design. I went to the museum in Santa Fe to see the old Jemez pots but it's just simple lines. I would rather do my own designs. It's all up here in my head. I use corn designs because I'm in the corn clan."

Juanita makes pottery and figurines painted with soft colors: tans and gray-blues and chalky whites. But she is best known for her melon bowls, a form she introduced to Jemez, slipped with a gray clay that fires to buff. She sculpts ribs on a wide variety of pots, from jars to wedding vases. "The big ones I push out from inside and groove them on the outside. Some I just sculpt on the outside. I have a new one I call my 'oval melon,' grooved only on one side.

"I'm always experimenting with anything I can get from Mother Earth," she says. "For melon bowls I use just a little more clay so it's easier to polish. If there is too much volcano ash, it won't stand up; if I use too much clay, then it's hard to sand. I have a new gold slip but it is hard to polish."

Kiowa writer N. Scott Momaday spent his teenage years at Jemez, where his parents taught at the day school. Juanita Fragua credits Scott's father Al with teaching her "how to draw, how to mix the paints. I got all the straight lines from him." Scott described Jemez Pueblo in his memoir *The Names*: "The village lies in all seasons like a scattering of smooth stones in a wide fold of the sandy earth."

Less metaphorical "smooth stones," found in the river bed, polish Juanita's pots. She polishes with a new stone first to break it in, then with an older, smoother stone to smooth out the scratches left by the first. If the stone is *too* polished, it doesn't work as well. "It just picks up the clay."

Laura Gachupin had one polishing stone that had been handed down for generations. She lost it—somehow—and says she will never forgive herself. Her sister Maxine Toya says that polishing stones just seem to disappear in mysterious ways. Maxine and Laura work together, along with their mother,

Jemez potter Maxine Toya with her pottery figures, ready for painting.

Marie Romero, who made the first storyteller at Jemez, in 1968. Maxine says Laura is the innovator with paints, while she experiments with form. The new ideas are "constantly changing hands."

Maxine makes figures. "I like to do something different each time I pick up the clay. I start with a flat base and start coiling. No matter how small the figure, I always coil and build it up to whatever I have in my mind. It's somewhere back there, ready to come out. So I have simplified my figures. I want to achieve the balance between traditional and contemporary."

Her pots resemble sculpture, with clay blankets that flow around the figures of flute players, singers, corn maidens, and mothers with children. "People tell me that my pieces look like me. That makes sense: they are a part of you. Whatever you have put into that piece, it has helped make you a better person. Your hand sort of flows through the piece. When you are done, and you hold it in your hands, to me they come alive."

Evelyn Vigil's recreation of Pecos-style glaze-painted pottery in its ancestral home at the ruins of Pecos Pueblo. (Pecos National Monument collection)

Maxine and her family started with poster paints and acrylics painted after firing. "But we wanted to make the pottery uniquely traditional, uniquely Jemez. We felt we were artists and we had a job to do. It was a releasing. Our whole attitude had to be changed."

Beginning with the two basic colors, rust-brown and black, they slowly developed their paints. Maxine says, "They come from the earth. They're for everyone in the community to use. It's something we shouldn't lose." She teaches fifth grade, and now she takes her classes to the clay and temper sites. "How are the children going to learn if we don't share the talents that we have? We're not taking it with us to wherever we are going."

Evelyn Vigil also worries about passing on what she has learned. And she has learned something remarkable. With the encouragement of the National Park Service at Pecos National Monument, this Jemez potter has recreated the old Pecos pottery painted with lead-based glaze.

Pecos people joined their linguistic relatives at Jemez when they abandoned Pecos in 1838. No one knows anymore who is related to the seventeen Pecos immigrants. As Evelyn says, they are "all mixed in." Pecos was one of the last strongholds of Pueblo glaze-painted pottery. Pueblo potters never glazed whole vessels, but from about 1250 until the technique disappeared about 1700, they painted designs on pottery with lead-based paint that melted to a shiny glaze in firing.

To recreate the old vessels, Evelyn searched around Pecos for clay, temper, and paint pigments. It took months, but she found the materials. She even found the place where the Pecos women had ground their sandstone temper: the metates were still there. But even then, she had to experiment with firing techniques that would be hot enough to melt the lead in her paint. That turned out to be the hardest part of the puzzle to piece together. "I tried cedar, straw, manure, and none worked. I tried cottonwood bark, and that didn't work. Finally I used fir bark, and that is the only thing that will work."

She ground her paint from lead ore (galena) mixed with guaco. Pure lead without guaco, sand, or alkali requires a hotter fire to melt and tends to run. At first, the galena came from Pecos; afterwards, from Cerrillos. Red iron yielded her other color. But grinding her own galena turned out to be "kind of dangerous—it jumps at you when you grind it." Evelyn decided she would have to buy her galena already ground.

In recreating the tradition of a whole pueblo, Evelyn Vigil symbolizes the powerful freedom of Jemez Pueblo potters to invent any style they want to. Now that Evelyn has learned this ancient skill, she wants to teach it to another generation of Jemez potters, but she says "no one is interested in learning. I'm going to try as long as I can to do these things. You are never lonesome as long as you have clay. When I leave this world maybe no one will do it. I'm just so anxious to teach somebody. I don't want to lose everything that I know, that I've learned. I am a person that believes in old things."

Clay Made from History: Acoma, Laguna, and Zuni

IF TIME-TRAVELING ANASAZIS walked into an Indian art gallery on the plaza in Santa Fe or Albuquerque, many things would mystify them. Some of the pottery, however, would look reassuringly familiar: orange Hopi vessels, plain cooking jars from Taos, and above all, black-on-white and corrugated pottery from Acoma.

Part of Acoma's heritage (along with that of other Keresans) lies in the abandoned villages of Chaco Canyon and Mesa Verde. The old pueblo on top of the mesa at Acoma—"Sky City"—dates from the 1200s or earlier. If you walk up the old trail worn into the side of the mesa and stand by one of the rock cisterns, the sight of a shawled woman passing between the weathered adobe houses takes you from the twentieth century to the eleventh.

Today only a few families live year round at Sky City. Most Acomas live in newer houses in the farming communities of Acomita, San Fidel, and McCartys, strung along the Santa Fe Railroad and Interstate 40 on the floodplain of the Rio San José.

Acoma's neighbor Laguna, just to the east, was a traditional Acoma farming area until the 1690s, when after the Pueblo Rebellion, refugees from several

Left, *Lucy Lewis decorating Acoma pottery*; above, *Acoma water jar made by Lucy Lewis in 1963 (Richard M. Howard collection).*

villages established Laguna Pueblo. In language, customs, and pottery, they have always maintained close ties with Acoma. A political split in the late 1800s sent displaced Lagunas to Isleta, south of Albuquerque, and Isleta pottery has been influenced by Laguna's pottery ever since.

Still farther west lies Zuni, with its unique language and distinctive ceremonial tradition. Together, Acoma, Laguna, Zuni, and Hopi make up the Western Pueblos. Hopi has its own pottery traditions; the other three have much in common, and their parallel traditions can be seen in the bold abstractions and rosettes of their pottery.

Hard Clay and Thin Walls

Acoma clay is special. Dark gray and nearly as dense as shale, it must be ground to a powder before being mixed with temper. Clean, soak, dry, crumble, sift, grind, and soak again; the hours add up fast. And if a potter does not take sufficient care—if she "rushes the clay," in Stella Shutiva's words—the surface of the fired pot will pit as tiny bits of alkali absorb moisture and spall off.

Acoma clay has the same pitting problems as Zia clay does, and these flaws have nothing to do with the skill of the potters. Some clays pit worse than others. Some potters minimize the problem with special cleaning techniques; some have concluded that kiln firing prevents pitting; some have even resorted to commercial clays, feeling they have no choice when collectors refuse to buy Acoma pots because of pitting.

More and more Acoma potters are buying molded pottery ("greenware") and painting it for kiln firing. Stella Shutiva says, "They don't know how much they are throwing their art away. They are good artists. I feel bad when I see someone putting a fine traditional design on junk." But the traditional ways continue. Grace Chino says, "I don't want to be a cheater." Juana Leno sums up her own reasons for taking the long route: "I want to make pottery out of my own hands—create something that somebody else will enjoy."

Stella Teller, from Isleta, watches with amazement as the Acomas mold their clay: "It's so durable, they can pull it paper thin." Lillian Salvador, an Acoma potter who makes some of the thinnest of Acoma jars, does not sand her pots. Her completed walls come from shaping and scraping the wet clay. She says, "You just want to keep on and on. Sometimes it gets too thin and then it starts cracking or getting out of shape. And then I say it's time to quit."

Acomas use ground pottery sherds for temper, recycling pieces of their own pottery that popped in firing. They also collect sherds from ruins at the base of the mesa, where, as Juana Leno says, "long time ago some ladies fired their

This Acoma water jar, made in the 1890s and now in the collection of the School of American Research, inspired Rose Chino Garcia to make the piece in the foreground in 1985. (School of American Research collection)

pottery." The broken pots were themselves made with ground sherds, so today's pottery may contain several generations of pots within its clay.

Grinding both the clay and the sherds makes for hard work. At other pueblos, the potters often say that sanding is the hardest part of their job. At Acoma, they say that preparing the clay is. Lillian Salvador persuades her husband, Wayne, to do the grinding for her. Stella Shutiva and her daughter Jackie Histia hire a friend to grind clay with a corn grinder hitched to a washing machine motor. Anasazi sherds bought from Navajos from "up around Crownpoint" are even more difficult to grind because they were tempered with sand, and probably require even more work than grinding Zia basalt.

From fully prepared and mixed clay, Acoma potters make large water jars famous for their thin, hard-fired walls. White slip goes on with a rag (Stella Shutiva says old T-shirts and flannel work best). After stone-polishing this surface, the artists paint complex polychrome abstractions, swirling red bands, flowers, and parrots. The Acoma parrot seems exotic, but parrots still occurred in the wild in southern New Mexico in the early years of the twentieth century. Even today, Pueblo people keep them for their feathers, to be used on ceremonial costumes.

Pottery ready for firing by Acoma's Grace Chino.

The birds are powerful symbols. To an Acoma steeped in tradition, parrots may symbolize the zenith and its clouds; the nadir, ancestors, and death; or the south and the sun. Likewise, the color red is connected with the south, the sun, summer, and fertility. An Acoma potter may paint a red parrot on a water jar simply because "that's the way it's done," but even if she does not consciously think about meanings and metaphors, all these symbols underlie the "old way."

Many potters who specialize in smaller shapes or even owls and nativities also make classic large water jars. Lolita Concho and her sister Frances Torivio use up to five colors: white, black, and three shades of red. Like so many potters, they started after their mother died, when they wondered what to do with her tools.

At eighty-two, Frances says, "We learned it the hard way, my sister and I, there was no one to teach us. Now I don't know how long I'll be making big potteries. I'm getting where I'm getting tired. Especially in painting, because it's awful hard to hold a big one. I'm not steady any more. But I'm glad that my children are learning. I've taught young ladies like my daughter Lilly Salvador. Oh, I just love her pottery. Her potteries are much thinner than mine. I don't know how she does it."

The paints take time to prepare, too, mixing the ground black mineral base with boiled-down beeweed. And finding the paint rocks is even more of a challenge than finding clay. Juana Leno and her family go up in the mountains in search of the dense, black, iron-rich hematite they use for paint pigment. "You just have to look for them, pick one up and try it out, rub it on a rock. No, this one's too sandy . . . then look some more."

Dolores Lewis Garcia stresses how worthwhile all this work is when she talks to her children about making traditional pottery: "Why be lazy to go get the clay? Why be lazy to go get the paints? All we have to do is go up there and get it, bring it home. Why spend more money on it when everything is there my Mother Nature provided? That's what art is all about, you have to work hard to get where you are today."

Acoma canteen by Marie Z. Chino. (Heard Museum collection)

Rediscovering the Ancestors

The Acomas are noted for their revival of prehistoric pottery styles. Those Anasazis browsing in galleries would find corrugated ware much like their own cooking pots, Mimbres bowls like the ones used in eleventh-century burials by Mogollon people in southern New Mexico, and many abstract black-on-white designs from Mesa Verde, Chaco Canyon, and the country around Reserve and Tularosa, south of Acoma.

Juana Leno's favorite designs are the swirling spirals called Tularosa by archaeologists—now a family design, particularly when painted on three-chambered canteens like the one her mother first made in the late 1800s. "She used that pot for her wedding. She used to store cornmeal in there, then water. Dr. Kenneth Chapman from Santa Fe came around looking for potsherds, and my mother sold that pot to him to send me to school, to buy shoes and clothing for me. She sold it for fifty dollars."

Stella Shutiva, with a corrugated Acoma jar, and her daughter, Jackie Histia, holding one of her own pots.

Stella Shutiva credits her mother, Jessie Garcia, with reviving corrugated pottery. "I just adored her corrugated. When I started up again making pottery, I wondered if I could ever do it. If I just watch Mom, it's hard to learn my own way. So I had to do it myself. It took almost four years."

Today, corrugated pottery in the "Shutiva style" is a family trademark. Stella's daughter Jackie Histia is making storytellers that sit on a corrugated plaque like her Grandmother Shutiva's braided rug, where Jackie sat to hear stories when she was a child. She molds her storyteller with a traditional dress but "brings it up to this generation" by clothing her pottery children in numbered football jerseys. Jackie's turtle storytellers are corrugated on top, "like the turtle's shell."

Prehistoric potters pinched each coil with their fingers as it was made, one coil at a time. For today's corrugated pots, each coil is left unsmoothed on the outside, and then textured all at once with a pointed tool when the pot is completed. The coils must be made precisely, without mistakes. On Lillian Salvador's corrugated miniatures, she rolls her coils so fine they are "almost like spaghetti." Someone once accused Stella Shutiva of using a cake decorator to texture her corrugated pottery. Now when she brings in her new pots, she tells the trader, with a smile, "This is all I could bring: my cake decorator broke."

Stella's family still keeps water in traditional jars in the summertime because it gives drinking water "a certain taste." Daughter Jackie "can drink and drink" from the pottery jars. "You never want to stop."

Dazzling fine-line designs have become another Acoma trademark. Mary Ann Hampton says she has to paint them in stages "because I start getting crosseyed." Many potters make the fine-line pots, but the late Marie Z. Chino, Lucy Lewis, and their families made them famous. Tight, narrow lines cover the pots in interlocking frets and hachures based on bits of potsherds and Anasazi pots in museum collections, but reinterpreted and personalized by modern Acoma women. Lucy's eyes are beginning to weaken, but she still paints using glasses. Her daughters Emma and Dolores say, "We can't do that fine-line, she's the one."

Marie Chino's daughters carry on her designs. Grace Chino says, "I don't copy from books, I just do like my mother. I took over the vase with the stepped design. When I paint it, I start it off with a little piece of straight paper to make it straight. I do that so it comes out even. I use my yucca brushes—I can't work with those commercial brushes."

Mimbres animals have become almost synonymous with Acoma since Kenneth Chapman encouraged modern potters to revive them. The Lewis family has been using these designs for more than twenty years, and many other Acoma potters paint them, as well. Rebecca Lucario makes particularly finely painted pieces.

Archaeologists have excavated thousands of Mimbres bowls from burials along the Mimbres River in southwestern New Mexico. Bowls with a hole punched through the bottom were placed over the head of the dead, leaving

Detail of an Acoma jar by Dorothy Torivio. (Heard Museum collection)

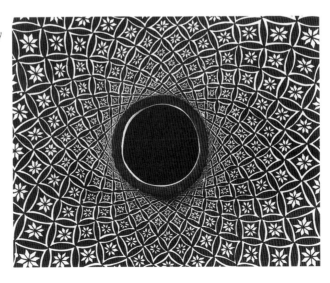

a path for the spirit to pass through to the next world. Mimbres people painted this remarkable pottery from A.D. 950 to 1150. They may seem ancient to us, but only six lifetimes separate them from historic Pueblo potters—not so long for an oral tradition.

As Acoma is the bridge between Rio Grande and Western Pueblo culture, it is also the bridge between prehistory and the present. Lillian Salvador puts it this way: "We all came from one place. As people traveled they spread. So our ancestors, some of them went down to the Mimbres valley. We all just carried our designs, they were passed down to us.

"We have a friend down there in the Mimbres Valley with a ruin on his land. We spent a whole day there. It made me feel so good—like we were at home and they were there, too. Although we couldn't see them, I felt that we were all just talking to each other. When I got home I went and sat down and started painting, and my animals just came out. We pounded the pottery sherds we picked up down there and I mixed it in with my clay and it just made me feel so good."

Rebecca Lucario painted these Acoma seed jars with Mimbres-style animals. (Wheelwright Museum Shop)

*Laguna water jar by
Gladys Paquin. (School of
American Research collection)*

The Power of Individualists: Laguna and Isleta

Historic Laguna pottery did not become recognizably different from Acoma pottery until about 1830. During the next century, the Lagunas perfected a variation of white-slipped polychrome with bold and simple designs, often banding the pot with broad stripes and hearts of red.

Pottery almost died at Laguna in the mid-twentieth century. Evelyn Cheromiah started making the old designs a few years ago, and she was joined in 1980 by Gladys Paquin.

Gladys embodies the complicated history of people and styles in today's pueblos. Born at Laguna, half Zuni, she was raised at Santa Ana. She lived in California for twenty-seven years before returning to Laguna, when, as she says, "The Lord Jesus put a desire in me to make pottery. He got me from nothing and made me a potter. Pottery is a lot like your relationship with God. God molds you and makes you and puts you in the fire."

Gladys began by making pots "inspired by my life. The story on one pot was the Song of David. Another one I've kept, it has a butterfly—I was a worm and the Lord came and changed me. The stairsteps mean the new dimension I found."

Pottery dealers in Santa Fe and specialists at the Wheelwright Museum and the School of American Research convinced Gladys she needed a "bridge from the old pottery" to hers. So she began making "copies" of old Laguna designs. "First I used the word 'copy,' now I think of carrying on their traditions, their inspiration. They were individuals just like me. One drew hearts, one drew something else. I can't believe it when they say that's traditional. I think it's just their inspiration—I wonder what this person thought about when they drew these things. I wonder what inspired this person to put these hearts on the pot."

Gladys learned the traditional ways on her own. She started with sherds as temper, but switched to volcanic ash. "The hardest part was learning how to fire, to control the fire, to know the fire. I pray to the Lord to have a hand on that pot. Firing is so hard, but my heart tells me one of these days it will pay off."

Gladys has taken her pots to the kiln to burn off black smoke clouds from ground firing, but the kiln-fired pottery turns orange instead of red. "It looks dead, it doesn't look alive to me. The kiln sort of kills it and dries it out. When it's done outside, it looks alive. That's why I stay away from the kiln.

"A real potter comes from the heart. I ask people to collect clay and grind sherds before they come talk to me about how to mold. If they can't go through the whole process, they don't have it on their heart to do it. I'm not stingy with information, but unless they care they won't really work."

Gladys Paquin dreams of having time to experiment with other clays she has found. "I would like to make the things that I'm led to make. I've become a slave to my bills, and the old designs helped me through. But I would like to get back to my own, to have something of myself.

"I don't live outrageous, I just live peaceable. I've never been so happy in my life."

At Isleta, Stella Teller has some of the same feelings about inspiration and tradition. Isleta's pottery was plain red until Laguna people settled there in 1880, introducing a black-and-red painted whiteware. Isleta potters made small bowls in this style, mostly to sell at the railroad station in Albuquerque. Stella remembers her mother using an old set of mattress springs for a firing grate, covering the single-bed-sized springs with little pots.

When Stella made the transition from commercial pots to traditional pots some twenty years ago, she developed her own style. Since she and her family are the most active traditional potters at Isleta, Isleta Pueblo pottery evolves in whatever direction Stella Teller's personal style develops. She now mixes her paints with the same white slip she uses to cover her pots. The lighter tones have a softness that contrasts with the turquoise that Stella inlays in some pieces.

She also makes figurines—nativity scenes and "corn doll" figures, Mother Corn with a bowlful of ears of corn. Stella finds figurines harder to fire than jars. She uses more volcanic ash temper for them and makes her molding mixture "clayier" for bowls "that will be stretched up."

Stella Teller, Isleta potter.

Stella's daughters make pottery, too. Robin, the oldest, was "the last to come to clay, but you can't get her to answer the phone now." Lynette, the youngest, mixes clay for the whole family, taking a commission on all their sales. Stella says, "It's a strenuous job, and she is the strongest one.

"I am proud of my pueblo," she declares, "but I think of my pottery as Stella Teller pottery more than Isleta pottery, since it's my own style and the design ideas come from museum pieces, not from Isleta. Really, all the pueblos use the same motifs; they are individualized by the potters."

But the materials and the spirit are Isleta. "From my great-grandmother on down were potters. My polishing stones came down from them. I'm *always* in the mood to make pottery. I'll never retire, I'll just keep making pottery and traveling until I'm an old woman."

Jenny Laate, pottery teacher at Zuni High School.

Rain Birds and Heart Lines

The Pueblo people know that the ceremonial cycle ties together the fabric of their world, and the same cycle also keeps pottery alive. Even when utilitarian pieces are no longer made at a pueblo and commercial art pottery has not started, the kiva leaders still need ceremonial vessels. A few stew bowls must be made for carrying food to the gods. Rain priests need canteens to carry water from the sacred springs.

At Zuni, pottery reached this miniscule level of output not long ago (Zuni potter Randy Nahohai attributes this to "too much Tupperware"), but two families—the Bicas and the Nahohais—kept making a few pieces, and pottery teachers in the school system introduced young Zunis to the art. Most of the high school students made a few small pots, gave them to their families, and that was that, but a few talented artists continued working after graduation.

In the 1930s, the teachers were Zuni women. In more recent years, two non-Zuni teachers have been the "pottery elders" of the pueblo: first Daisy Hooee

Nampeyo, a Hopi-Tewa married to a Zuni man; and since 1974, Jenny Laate, an Acoma married into Zuni.

Daisy taught the students, "Do your best in school, even though you are behind. Never give up. That's the only way." She and Jenny both teach the children Zuni designs, using pictures of old pots in books. Though the classes sometimes have used commercial clay and now fire the pots in electric kilns, Jenny has tried to keep her students supplied with local clay. She makes two collecting trips each year, each yielding about two hundred pounds of clay before mixing with sandstone temper. The janitor at the school told her where to go to find the clay—and made sure she prayed. For her own pottery, she sometimes ground-fires at the family sheep ranch.

Beginning students must make three pieces in six weeks. Intermediate students move on to bowls, owls, and miniatures. Jenny says, "My boys turn out better than the girls. Girls get discouraged too fast." Her best-known pupil is Anderson Peynetsa, and four or five other students have continued to pot after leaving her class.

Zuni owls can be made several ways. Jenny Laate makes the body as a closed sphere, keeping the air inside so it won't collapse. Finally, at the very end of the process, she pierces the nose, opening up the owl before firing. Rowena Nahohai makes a hole in her owls earlier, blowing gently into the body if she needs to fix a dent and attaching the wings and beak with small pieces of clay. Her mother-in-law, Josephine, makes her owls from thicker slabs of clay and pinches out the wings, beak, and ears from the body. Josephine says that the owl "is the protector of the night, always on the lookout for your family and making sure that your family is safe."

Another classic Zuni design is the deer standing "in its house," with a heart-line piercing its body. The white space around the heart-line is the entrance trail of the deer's life-breath. Daisy Hooee tells why "the Zuni deer is on that pot, when it looks funny there. It's because there's no water anywhere around where the Zunis landed" when they arrived in this world. A deer led them to water, and "everybody was happy that they found the water with that deer. So that's the reason they put the deer right there on the water pot."

Water animals—tadpoles, dragonflies, and frogs—decorate ceremonial vessels: cornmeal bowls with stepped sides, terraced like clouds. Hatching means rain; feathers imply prayersticks and prayers. Black and white checkerboards represent the Milky Way. For Daisy Hooee, the designs are stories reflecting a world full of stories. She looks at the stars and sees "a lot of stories up there."

Josephine Nahohai switched from jewelrymaking to potterymaking so she wouldn't have to buy silver and turquoise. "All you have to do is just to get

The Nahohai family of Zuni: Josephine, her sons, Milford and Randy, and Randy's wife, Rowena. Milford holds a jar painted with the Zuni rain bird; Randy holds baby J.C. — perhaps the next generation in Zuni potterymakers.

the clay and make the pottery." She talked with Daisy and she talked with her aunt: "That's how I learn it." At first her husband did the painting, but now the whole family is involved.

In 1985 Josephine received a Katrin H. Lamon artist's fellowship from the School of American Research to help teach traditional potterymaking to other Zunis. She and her family brought several potters with them to the School's research collection in Santa Fe to study old pottery. Three of the women were Zuni Olla Maidens, members of a social dance group who sing traditional Zuni songs as they dance with Zuni water jars balanced on their heads. Once, when the Zuni women took a break while working in the School's collections, each chose her favorite pot off the shelves and paraded happily around the vault with the piece in its traditional, rightful place—on her head. The curator of the collection walked in on this scene—to his delight (and concern!).

These students of the old designs started with copying, but they never *just* copy. Says Josephine's son Randy, "Every time I mix around the designs so that they are all original, my own interpretations of what the old designs meant."

Randy's favorite designs are the "rain birds," an abstracted swirling spiral (sometimes identified as a rattlesnake) that has been used on Zuni pots for more than a century. His wife, Rowena, makes mostly owls, bears, and duck canteens. Brother Milford paints, too. As they go along, they discover and rediscover what Zuni potters have been learning and relearning for centuries.

Randy knows that "you have to mix your paint really right. If you don't mix it right—you add too much stone—it will just rub off. If you add too much of that wild spinach, it just cracks off or flakes off." He laments the work of potters who don't learn "the beliefs behind the painting."

An example is the "line break"—deliberately leaving incomplete one or more of the lines encircling a pot. Pueblo potters have used the line break off and on for at least a thousand years, and its original meaning has evolved with time. Randy believes "that line is a representation of your own life. If you meet it together you end your own life." Daisy Hooee says the line break has to do with "long life, children, healthy people." Some women leave the line open if they still can bear children, close it if they cannot. Others say that two lines must be left broken, one for the spirit of the pot to enter the vessel, one for it to escape.

Traditions change. Meanings evolve. Together, the Nahohais and their students are rediscovering, refining, and rejuvenating Zuni pottery.

CHAPTER SIX

The Legacy of Sikyatki: Hopi

T HE LONG-ABANDONED Hopi pueblo of Sikyatki left a legacy: a tradition of fine pottery that still gives vitality to Hopi potterymaking. Today's Hopi potters do not use the old designs by rote, but they find them an endless source of inspiration.

Arizona's Hopi villages are the only modern pueblos not in New Mexico, a separation expressed in many ways. Hopis speak a language related to that of Great Basin Indian people. Their ceremonies are more concerned with bringing rain to their arid home than New Mexico Pueblo ceremonies (one Tewa describes Hopi ceremonies as esoteric and magical "weather-control"). And the Hopis lived in isolation longer than any other Pueblo group, removed from both their Pueblo kin and the influences of Spanish and Anglo colonists. As a result, Hopi traditions have remained strong.

After the Pueblo Revolt in 1680 and the Spanish reconquest in 1692, a group of Tewa people who had lived near Santa Fe abandoned their pueblo and moved to Hopi. Tradition has it that the Hopis invited them, for the Tewas had a reputation as fierce warriors, and the less aggressive Hopis wanted their help in dealing with Ute raiders. The Tewas settled in a single village on First Mesa called Hano or simply Tewa Village, and they have lived as a

Left, Sikyatki bird motifs swirling on a jar by Hopi-Tewa Dextra Quotskuyva (Richard M. Howard collection); above, Hopi whiteware wedding vase by Joy Navasie (Heard Museum collection).

Golden Hopi jar by Stella Huma. (Richard M. Howard collection)

minority within Hopi society ever since. After almost three hundred years, the Hopi-Tewas remain separate from both their Hopi neighbors and their distant Tewa kin.

In the old days, every Hopi village made pottery. Gradually, the mesas have come to specialize in their crafts: Third Mesa, wicker baskets; Second Mesa, coiled baskets; First Mesa, pottery. A few potters at Third Mesa continue to make unpainted pottery. But in all three of the First Mesa villages—Walpi, Sichomovi, and Hano, as well as the modern village of Polacca at the base of the mesa—most women make pottery.

Five Generations of Nampeyo's Stories

For six centuries distinctive orange pottery has come from the Hopi mesas. The trademark Hopi clay, gray before firing, can turn any shade from cream, buff, or yellow to apricot, peach, or light red, depending on its iron content and the firing (in a non-oxidizing fire, it even bakes to white). Higher firing temperatures, obtainable with local coal as fuel, yield the lightest colors. The surface of a single pot, polished unslipped or slipped with the same clay that it's made from, may grade through several of these colors. Golden Hopi pottery just may have given rise to the legends of golden vessels that drew Coronado and his Spaniards northward in 1540.

Quality of workmanship and creativity of design in prehistoric Hopi pottery climaxed between 1375 and 1625 in the style named for the village of Sikyatki, at the eastern base of First Mesa. The Sikyatki artisans introduced several painting methods, including spattering and stippling, using black paints (mixed from vegetal and mineral pigment) and red clay paints.

In the late 1800s, when these pots came to light again as archaeologists excavated the ruins of Sikyatki, Hopi potters had been making little of this traditional orange pottery. White-slipped pottery, with designs heavily influenced by Zuni (where many Hopis had moved to wait out drought and a smallpox epidemic in the 1860s), had mostly replaced it.

In the 1880s, a Tewa woman from Hano named Nampeyo and her husband Lesou, from Walpi, became intrigued with the Sikyatki designs they found on potsherds. The two formed a creative team that rivaled the later partnership of Maria and Julian Martinez of San Ildefonso. Maria and Nampeyo became the best-known of all Pueblo potters.

Like Maria's, Nampeyo's talent blossomed at a crucial time. Thomas Keam had opened a trading post for the Hopis in 1875, providing a market for pottery and a stock of coveted goods to be traded for. In the 1880s Keam commissioned copies of several prehistoric pottery styles, from plain and corrugated to Sikyatki, paying extra for fine work. Several potters evidently made copies for Keam, but we do not know for sure if Nampeyo was one of them. Nampeyo began using Sikyatki shapes and designs on her white-slipped pottery between 1885 and 1890. In the 1890s, archaeologists under Jesse Walter Fewkes excavated Sikyatki, and dozens of the exquisite vessels came from the ruin. Lesou worked on the excavation team. By 1900 Nampeyo had fully revived the Sikyatki style, rediscovering the Sikyatki clay sources, abandoning white slip, and polishing the yellow body clay itself.

Although the old designs from Sikyatki and other ruins inspired Nampeyo, she distilled them through her own creativity. Her potteries were far more

The pioneering Hopi-Tewa potter Nampeyo. (Museum of New Mexico #36155)

than copies. The other women of First Mesa followed her lead, and with the encouragement of Fewkes's assistant Walter Hough and Keam's guarantee of a market, they brought about a renaissance in Hopi pottery.

Daisy Hooee learned potterymaking from Nampeyo, her grandmother, in those early years of the twentieth century and interpreted for her when visitors came until Nampeyo's death in 1942. She says, "In those days we don't have no pencils. We used charcoal. Whenever we bring a paper sack from the store we spread it out and that's where she copies the designs if she goes to the ruins." They stacked the pottery designs drawn on paper sacks "with a flat rock on top," and when Nampeyo made her big pots, "she would take one out and she'd copy that on her pottery."

Daisy says of Nampeyo's designs, "All the grandchildren now they're putting it on their pottery. We don't copy other tribes: it has to be a Hopi design. And when they buy from me I tell the stories that Nampeyo tells me."

Nampeyo's stories continue through the generations. Dextra Quotskuyva, Daisy's niece, says, "I feel good about doing the traditional designs of Nampeyo. I feel I'm closer to her because I'm using that design. Although she's gone, I feel that she's there."

The Nampeyo family designs combine scrolls of fine-line decoration with stylized birds and bird wings, beaks, and feathers. The best of them have such a feeling of motion that they seem ready to swirl away under their own power and fly right off the table. These new versions of the old Sikyatki designs also include animal forms: butterflies and birds, kachina faces, and a myriad of stylized animals that pottery specialists lump in the category of "zoomorphs."

The Sikyatki shapes are also distinctive: wide-shouldered flattened jars, often with an outflaring lip; low bowls with spectacular decoration inside; and seed jars with small openings in their center and flattened tops that seem to defy the laws of structural strength dictated by the clay. Other shapes that seem distinctly Hopi came from elsewhere. The wedding vase came from the Rio Grande. Tiles were commissioned by Thomas Keam, who provided molds to ensure their uniformity. And in 1922, Santa Fe writer Frank Applegate spent some time on the mesas helping potters. He encouraged them to make the tall, straight-sided vase that became a characteristic Hopi vessel. The largest ones, three feet high, were used as umbrella stands.

Designs from Dreams

Dextra Quotskuyva says, "Most of my designs are from the dreams that I had, from looking at the earth, everything in the universe." She still does the Nampeyo family designs that she made with her mother, but when she began making pottery on her own she wanted to include other designs, other "feelings," other dreams.

"With one I designed not very long ago I wanted you to not really look at it but *feel* it. I had represented the sun and the moon from both sides and then I looked at the sky, and to me the sky is smooth. Then looking at the ground—the sand, the rough places, the feeling of walking without shoes. . . . So I molded that pot, trying to make that pot look more like the world. Then I had the trail, just one trail, traveling and entering, going up, and not just the trail but the spirit of everything, everybody, everything that's leaving this earth."

Dextra designed another pot "with all the confusion of everybody, how you feel, but I left one place, left one opening, that I didn't fill in, just to show there is a way out for everybody. There's always hope.

"You worry about your pots; it's just like your children that you are bringing into the world. There's a lot of pots with meaning that went out without explanation because some don't really ask. But if they're not interested in explanation, I know what it means. I have that feeling and that's what it's talking about. If they just feel it, maybe they'll get closer to what I mean."

The old designs also have rich stories. Daisy Hooee remembers what Nampeyo said about her "volcano pot," tracing the colors and shapes of one she

Hopi-Tewa Daisy Hooee and her "volcano pot."

has made herself. "She said that this pot was shaped like a mountain. Red lava comes down. When the lava is still wet it comes down like that. And then he goes under and comes down here and is cooling off and the outside part is still. And these are the ashes. So they call it a volcano pot. Red is all around. This is the same that is on the ground, not cooling off yet, still red hot."

Dextra Quotskuyva encourages other Hopis and Hopi-Tewas to make pottery, "not just within our family." "There's just no sense in forgetting what was there before. Art helps other people; you can't really hold it to yourself. It has to go out."

Every family passes on designs through the generations. When Susanna Denet went to the Museum of Northern Arizona in Flagstaff, she was thrilled to be able to pick out her mother's pots from two rooms full of Hopi pottery.

"No one did the mouths like her. It made me cry to see those pots. We stood in silence for a while—it seemed so long—and then I pulled myself together and moved on. I carry her designs."

Grace Chapella was Nampeyo's next-door neighbor in Tewa Village. From among the Sikyatki bowls coming out of the excavation, Grace chose a butterfly pattern, added embellishments, and made it her own. She lived to be more than a hundred and taught her great-grandson Mark Tahbo, who carries on her designs. Just as his great-grandmother had done many years before, Mark worked as a cook at Polacca Day School. One payday, he came home to a check for a pot his family had sold for him. The pottery check was more than his salary check, so he quit his cooking job and began potting full time.

Rondina Huma, another Hopi-Tewa potter, has "a design that I made on my own. It's related to the Nampeyos' with fine lines, but a lot different from theirs, too. I used to make big designs and I used to leave some areas not painted. I was just doing it one day and I started from the top clear to the bottom and I find that it looks better with more designs on there than just leaving so many blank spaces. I want one of my daughters or my sister's kids to take over my work if they can, my style, and make their living for themselves out of that."

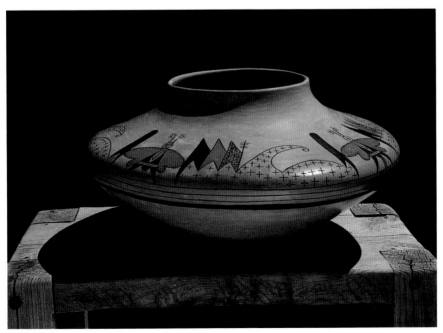

Grace Chapella's butterfly design on a pot made by her great-grandson Mark Tahbo. (Rick Dillingham collection)

Jar by Rondina Huma, Hopi-Tewa. (Rick Dillingham collection)

Yellow Clay, Red Pots, and White Slip

Tracy Kavena of Sichomovi says, "People ask me what the designs mean. I ask my grandma the same thing. She says to me, 'It's up to you to interpret. It's good to make up your own designs based on the old traditional elements.' " Modern Hopi potters have revived so many different prehistoric styles that they give pause to anthropologists trying to classify their pottery. One scientist noted that in the course of a year, a single Hopi family makes pottery that could be classified as twenty different styles.

Hopi potters use a gray clay to make yellow pottery and a yellow clay to make red pottery. The more iron in the clay, the redder the fired pot. Some potters use only a yellow slip to make red pottery, using the same slip for one color of polychrome paint.

Rondina Huma gathers her clay near the ruined village of Awatovi. The clay is so good, "it just shapes itself." She doesn't temper the Awatovi clay, "but other places, the clays are real rich. You have to add a little sand to it." Adding sand also makes it easier to sand the pottery. Other potters have fired plaques of white clay, ground them to flour, and used them as a very fine temper.

Susanna Denet likes to use extremely rich clay because she doesn't use a slip. She polishes only with rainwater: "You don't know what's in tap water." Other potters like coarse, sandy clay and tell her they can't work with her clay, that it's too rich and "will pop."

Sikyatki designs appear on red or golden pottery. Red pottery, particularly, is decorated with a host of simpler geometric designs, made mostly in Sichomovi. Susanna Denet uses black paint on red pottery and both black and red on yellow pots.

The late Garnet Pavatea popularized red bowls with a band of corrugation around the shoulder. Prehistoric potters used their fingernails to pattern corrugated vessels and she simulated this texture with the even imprints of a "church key"—a metal can opener. Other potters still make redware bean pots, stew bowls (complete with ladles), and mixing bowls to hold batter for the paper-thin Hopi *piki* bread, made of blue cornmeal. They use them, too. Susanna Denet has three ladles hanging next to her stove, one given to her by an aunt forty-eight years ago.

Two families, the Navasies and Nahas, have specialized in whiteware. Their most noted members are Frog Woman (Joy Navasie) and Feather Woman (Helen Naha). Firing the white clay is difficult. The pots need an extra hot fire. The Navasie family uses slates or slabs of asbestos instead of potsherds to protect the delicate white slip from smudging. Designs on the whiteware are often Sikyatki inspired, but some, particularly the Naha pots, are derived from more ancient black-on-white styles.

Red corrugated bowl by the late Garnet Pavatea. (Heard Museum collection)

The Naha family design — made by Sylvia,
this generation's Feather Woman.
(Richard M. Howard collection)

Sylvia Naha, Helen's daughter, first made pottery when she played with the adobe in her father's field below Awatovi. One day her father plowed up a pot with a swirling geometric design. Since then, it has become a Naha family design. Sylvia paints freehand, using yucca brushes for large pots, paintbrushes for small ones, and the butt of a wooden matchstick for stippling. She applies layer after layer of white slip until it is "eggshell thick," polishing only the last layer.

Her mother told her, "Never leave anything out, in your design or your process. Sand and polish as far as your fingers will reach." Sylvia polishes the insides of narrow jars with a nail or even her fingernail. She had a tiny polishing stone she used for miniatures—until her little boy accidentally swallowed it. She finds other polishing stones in gravel.

Rondina Huma believes white pottery is the hardest of all. "I tried it once but it's not my style." To use the white slip, "You have to be fast enough to polish that because it dries so fast. Then when you paint, the paint soaks in so fast." Sylvia Naha uses razor blades (her little cousin calls them her "erasers") to scrape off any mistakes made with the five or six clays she paints with. She must take care not to slice down into the slip, or the mark will show. One advantage of white pottery, however, is that the white slip reveals air bubbles, and the potter is rarely surprised by a "pop" in firing.

Sculptured corn on a vase by Hopi potter Polingaysi Qoyawayma (Elizabeth White). (Heard Museum collection)

Mother Corn

Third Mesa potter Polingaysi Qoyawayma (Elizabeth White) generated a unique style singlehandedly. In the early 1960s, Polingaysi began making unpainted, cream-colored pottery with the figure of an ear of corn pushed out from the inside and sculpted on the soft-hued side of her bowls. A pioneer Hopi teacher before she became a potter, Polingaysi wrote of the power of "Mother Corn," who "nourished the Hopi people" and with "her pollen pathway like a rainbow in the sky directed the Hopi to life."

Her nephew Al Qoyawayma has carried on her style, adding sculpted butterflies, Kokopeli the humpbacked flute player, kachinas, and blanketed Hopi men. Al comes to his pottery trained as an engineer. He lives in Scottsdale and has become a technical expert on Hopi and Anasazi pottery. Reaching for the limits of structural strength in his flattened Sikyatki shapes, he went back to the original ancient pieces and measured them. He found that the Sikyatki potters had been unable to make the shapes he had been unable to make. They too had been engineers.

Al Qoyawayma goes to Hopi to gather his materials. He has a sense of history. "As I climb over the mesas and through the washes looking for clay, I realize that there have been many before me who have taken the same steps and have made the same search—and have seen the same beauty. I know that some of this clay may even contain the dust of my ancestors—so—how respectful I must be. And I think, perhaps I too might become part of a vessel, some day! What a thought."

Every Hopi sees the world differently. Some women potters don't approve of men like Al Qoyawayma, Wallace Youvella, and Mark Tahbo making pottery. Others believe that men make the *best* potters.

Mark Tahbo has had no problems with such disapproval. When he gets together with women who pot, he "talks pottery." When he had a bad year for firing, with a dark mark repeatedly turning up that wouldn't burn off, he was almost ready to quit potting. Finally, he went across the road to Priscilla Namingha Nampeyo for advice. Together they concluded that the rusted old galvanized bucket Mark used for soaking was contaminating his clay. Priscilla told him to buy a plastic bucket. He did, and the problem was solved.

Another area of disagreement has to do with using kachina designs on pottery. It is done now, and it was done in Sikyatki times. Thomas Keam encouraged these pieces. But several potters believe it is not right because in firing, the kachina is burned, and one should not do such a thing.

Every potter has her own rules, her own designs, her own way. Rondina Huma says: "I guess if you know how to do your pottery a certain way, that's the only way you do it, and if you try it somebody else's way, it doesn't come out."

Independence grows from tradition. Daisy Hooee says proudly, "It's all by freehand. Everything. That's the way my grandmother Nampeyo taught me. Shiny stones—she gave these polishing stones to me. This is the rock for paint mixing that was hers too."

Tracy Kavena says, "We're all individuals and no two potters are going to make the same pottery. A part of their personality goes into the pot.

Hopi tiles with kachina faces by Sadie Adams and Lorna Lomakema.
(Richard M. Howard collection)

"My father has a big water jug that my grandmother carried from Oraibi to Hotevilla when they left. It sits in the bookcase by my father's bed. Sometimes I just look at it and think—someday I'll do something like that. It's part of family history. All the knowledge needs to be handed down because some-day *we'll* be the old people."

Dextra Quotskuyva remembers Nampeyo telling her and the other kids, " 'When you grow up and get older, do your potteries like me. You're going to survive on it.' At that time I didn't know what she meant. 'You're going to live with it.' I used to think, why is she telling us this? She was a wise old lady."

CONCLUSION

One with the Clay:
Economics and Tradition

H ER GRANDFATHER INSPIRED Helen Cordero's storyteller figures. "He was a wise man with good words, and he had lots of grandchildrens and lots of stories, and we're all in there, in the clay." Elizabeth White prays to be "One with the clay. One with the Creator. One with every living thing, including the grains of sand."

We are all in there, every living thing. The clay is connected to the rest of a potter's world, and as Dextra Quotskuyva says, to "everything in the universe." "Most of the time I'm in there talking to the pots," she says. "Indians always have too much to do—harvesting time, planting, dances, we're very involved in cooking and all that stuff. We are baking from maybe Wednesday on for some occasion. We have Indian doings. As much as you want to fill orders, you can't explain because they don't know what we do besides making potteries. It takes time to make pottery."

Dora Tse Pe Peña says, "When someone orders a pot, they think, you should have it by a certain day. You can say, I'll try. But with our way of life, we have things coming up that happen just like overnight. There's no warning ahead of time. One evening they can come and say, 'Okay, we want you at the kiva.'

Left, *Santa Fe's Indian market — including some 350 Pueblo potters — takes over the streets surrounding the plaza and the Palace of the Governors; above, Acoma parrot jar by Lillian Salvador.*

So you drop all your work and go to the kiva. So then your pot isn't going to be ready on the day that the person wants it. And that's really hard to make people understand.

"It's living in two worlds. I worry, because if it's that way now, I worry about what it's going to be when my children are grown and they have children and grandchildren. I hope they can cope with it."

Pueblo pottery is part of life. And Pueblo life is more than pottery. Nothing can be taken for granted. Being truly Hopi, for example, does not come automatically. Third Mesa elder, the late Percy Lomaquahu, explained: "Humbleness means peace, honesty—all mean Hopi. True, honest, perfect words—that's what we call Hopi words. In all the languages, not just in Hopi. We strive to be Hopi. We call ourselves Hopi because maybe one or two of us will become Hopi. Each person must look into their heart and make changes so that you may become Hopi when you reach your destination."

Words, stories, designs, pottery—all are part of being a Pueblo Indian. "The feeling of creating, the part of life that makes you happy and joyful, doesn't just stop at pottery for me," says Nora Naranjo-Morse. "I feel the same when I look at my kids or make a beautiful pie. These people that I come from, I know they felt that a long time ago. They didn't worry if they were going to fail. They didn't worry if the judges at Indian Market would like their work. That's what made that spirit inconquerable. It held its own. It still does."

Lillian Salvador says, "It's not complicated to me because that's what was left here for us. I don't know how to describe it. You have to be an Indian to really understand it." "It has to be that way," Mary Trujillo says of traditional pottery. "Our life is that way."

A Sacred Business

For Lois Gutierrez-de la Cruz, the hardest part of being a potter is "the business. Pricing is hard for me. Before Indian Market, my husband Derek and I will put all our pottery out and that's the hardest thing—trying to figure out how much we're going to charge for something. To be fair about it to the customer and to ourselves, as far as the time and the work we put into it.

"Every once in a while I get attached to a piece. But I can't hold on to every pot. Bills have to be paid. I enjoy it while I'm doing it. And I think that's the important thing, to enjoy what you're doing. If you don't, I think it shows in your work."

Derek adds, "When we first started out, Lois's mom, Petra, said, 'Okay, you're going to work on pottery, but you've got to do it the right way. You can't get greedy.' It's okay to make a living, it's okay to be good at it, but what she said was like a warning: 'Don't get crazy about it. Don't get greedy. Have respect for what you do.' "

Bernice Suazo-Naranjo says, "Sometimes I wish that I didn't need the money so that I could keep some of the pieces. But that's where some of the rewards come in: when someone else likes the piece you feel really good. I like to sell to collectors because you know that they are buying it for their own self and they will hoard the pot. It's a different feeling than selling to galleries or wholesalers."

Nora Naranjo-Morse describes Indian Market as a "group encounter session" in terms of what she can learn. "Some people just don't relate to my pieces, some keep looking and looking, coming back, trying to decide, 'What is it?' People need categories. It's almost as if things shouldn't be fun or playful. Children look at my work and nod; that's better than a ribbon.

"I get torn when it comes down to merchandise, when I have to put a price tag on that traditional feeling. I'll always look at my pottery before I take it to sell. It's like a football team huddling—my clay people and I, we give each other the last 'humph-hah!' and then we go for it."

Potters live in the present; they don't hoard the past. Pottery is meant to go out on its journey. Acoma potter Juana Leno says, "Sometimes you feel like you want to keep it—but if I don't give it away, what's the point of making it?" Experienced potters speak with glee of seeing their crude and crooked early pots in collections, almost as if someone else made them. They live in the present.

The potters speak of becoming lost in what they are doing, staying up until two or three in the morning working. Mary Cain says, "Sometimes I would sit there, busy, busy, busy, and I even forget to come in here to the kitchen and do the cooking for supper. On those days my family excuses me. Then they take me to McDonalds."

Gladys Paquin sometimes yearns for a "regular" job. "My mind tells me eight to five would be a lot easier. My heart tells me different."

Artisans and Artists

Few other Pueblo arts arouse such dedication. Pottery is the only one that provides a living that comes right out of the culture: silverwork, sculpture, and easel painting have less to do with the Pueblo tradition. Though some archaeologists persist in calling the revival of prehistoric pottery styles "decadence," others have pointed out that such a revival is a quiet statement of the worth of the past, of the importance of traditional values. Perhaps that is why there is such sadness among the older potters when they talk about the use of molded pottery, commercial paints and clays, and kiln firing.

A delicate balance exists between buyer and potter. Fire clouds and pitting make pottery undesirable to many consumers, so the Indian women reluctantly resort to kiln firing to solve these problems. When collectors then refuse to buy their pottery because it has been kiln fired, they are caught in the middle of irreconcilable demands.

Juana Leno steadfastly follows the traditional Acoma ways. Her son operates a commercial ceramic supply at the pueblo. She put her foot down when he wanted to make a mold of her personal hallmark, the three-chambered canteen. She told him that if he did, he "would put me out of business." He did not make the mold.

Interaction between tradition and the marketplace cannot be ignored. Potters still pray to Clay Woman before they make their pots, but they make their living from the work as well. Some skilled Pueblo potters paint molded "ceramics" because they believe they can make better wages by doing so.

One historian of Pueblo pottery distinguishes between artisans and artists. The latter are the conscious innovators, and the innovations have been happening for centuries. So has the business. Just before Americans introduced factory-made vessels to the Southwest in the mid-1800s, Pueblo potters were making pieces to supply forty thousand New Mexico settlers—in addition to pots made for their own use. They traded pottery for goods in those days. Now they sell their work.

Some 150,000 people came to Santa Fe Indian Market in 1985. They spent twenty-three million dollars in the town during market week. Four million dollars of the total went directly to the Indian people exhibiting at the market, where the average participant earned two-thirds of his or her annual income in that single August weekend. The potters speak time and again of trying to save their best pieces for Indian Market, for the Hopi Craftsman Show at the Museum of Northern Arizona, or for the Eight Northern Pueblos Show. But these days, buyers come to their homes year round. It's hard to save a pot when it will sell immediately for a good price.

And potters clearly pay attention to what their customers want. They keep tabs on the marketplace quietly, mostly by their own experience of what sells and what does not. Wayne Salvador knows his wife Lilly's Mimbres pots will do well at the Heard Museum because the Heard had a Mimbres exhibit recently, and people there "recognize that type of art." Stella Teller says nativity scenes sell best at Santa Fe Indian Market, corn dolls best in Arizona;

Europeans always buy the most expensive pots, Texans the biggest. The Nahohai family says bear figurines go fast in California.

The potter's world is ever widening. Unpredictable new problems arise, too. Stella Teller sometimes has to refire her pots to burn off the greasy, sticky fingerprints left by people at shows who have been eating fry bread and honey. The line break seems to be dying out because buyers think it makes the design look unfinished.

Even with such concerns, many potters keep to themselves. A woman living in a cinderblock house a quarter mile from an old adobe pueblo talks about her friends who live "down at the pueblo," as if they lived miles and miles away. Most potters say they pay no attention to anyone else's work. Many live up to that; some say a jealous word or two, accusing others of using commercial clays or paints, painting molded "greenware," or even sanding off the name from the bottom of a pot and signing their own.

Some tribal leaders and other potters get upset with Indians who give demonstrations at museum shows or teach pottery workshops to non-Indians, giving away "secrets." Every potter who takes such a step must ask herself why she does so. Susanna Denet "used to see my people cut down to nothing in price, and I wanted to do something to help my people. I demonstrate to educate the outsiders, so that they will know what goes into the potteries." Her family supports her decision. "If my children hadn't done so much," she says, "I wouldn't be where I am. They work with me and they brought a lot of credit to me; I'm really proud of them."

The Pueblo women recognize commercial shortcuts because they make the pottery look "too perfect." Though many of them strive for perfection, they always compare pottery to people, and since people are not perfect, pottery can be the same way and still be valid.

Dora Tse Pe Peña is afraid that "one day potterymaking is going to go. I tell my girls, 'I feel good that I'm helping keeping it going. And I want you to do the same thing.' They are following my advice. And I hope they always will."

Notes on Sources

QUOTATIONS FROM POTTERS throughout the text come primarily from interviews I conducted with Pueblo artists in 1984–1986. The originals of taped interviews are now in the archives of the School of American Research, Santa Fe. I acknowledge the Heard Museum, Phoenix, for permission to quote from my interviews with Bessie Namoki, Blue Corn, Rose Naranjo, and Jody Folwell.

Published sources used for quotes from potters include Barbara Babcock's work on Helen Cordero (see note below for Middle Rio Grande chapter); Ruth Bunzel, *The Pueblo Potter* (Dover Reprint, 1929); *Al Qoyawayma: Hopi Potter* (Santa Fe East, 1984); Rick Dillingham, "Nine Southwestern Indian Potters," *Studio Potter* 5, no. 1 (Summer 1976); Alice Marriott, *Maria: The Potter of San Ildefonso* (University of Oklahoma Press, 1948); "Southwestern Pottery Today," *Arizona Highways* (May 1974); and an interview with Nathan Youngblood by Jaap VanderPlas, *Artlines* (August 1985).

In the following notes, author-date citations refer to works previously cited.

Introduction: The People

The primary source on southwestern Indians, both prehistoric and contemporary, is the *Handbook of North American Indians*, vol. 9, *Southwest* (Alfonso Ortiz, editor, Smithsonian Institution, 1979). The prehistoric Pueblo story told here comes mostly from Linda S. Cordell's *Prehistory of the Southwest* (Academic Press, 1984) and the less technical book by Dewitt Jones and Linda S. Cordell, *Anasazi World* (Graphic Arts Center, 1985).

For more detail on modern Pueblo Indians, see Edward P. Dozier, *The Pueblo Indians of North America* (Holt, Rinehart and Winston, 1970). Alfonso Ortiz explores Pueblo world view in *The Tewa World* (University of Chicago Press, 1969) and in *New Perspectives on the Pueblos* (University of New Mexico Press, 1972).

Talking With the Clay: Technique

In addition to Bunzel (1929), for more information on the techniques of Pueblo potters see Alfred E. Dittert, Jr., and Fred Plog, *Generations in Clay: Pueblo Pottery of the American Southwest* (Northland Press, 1980); Betty LeFree, *Santa Clara Pottery Today* (University of New Mexico Press, 1975); Marjorie F. Lambert, *Pueblo Indian Pottery: Materials, Tools, and Techniques* (Museum of New Mexico Press, 1966); and Carl E. Guthe, *Pueblo Pottery Making* (Yale University Press, 1925). The story about the Albuquerque psychiatrist comes from Susan Peterson's *Lucy M. Lewis: American Indian Potter* (Kodansha, 1984).

Mountain Villages: Taos and Picuris

Published sources concerning Taos- and Picuris-style pottery are meager. See Francis H. Harlow, *Modern Pueblo Pottery 1880-1960* (Northland Press, 1977) for the basics.

The Red and the Black: Tewa Pueblos

The story of Maria comes from Marriott (1948); Richard L. Spivey, *Maria* (Northland Press, 1979); and Susan Peterson, *The Living Tradition of Maria Martinez* (Kodansha, 1977). See also Kenneth M. Chapman, *The Pottery of San Ildefonso Pueblo* (University of New Mexico Press, 1970); Nancy Fox, "Rose Gonzales," *American Indian Art Magazine* (Autumn 1977, pp. 52–57); and the Maxwell Museum of Anthropology's *Seven Families in Pueblo Pottery* (University of New Mexico Press, 1974).

The most complete source on Santa Clara is LeFree (1975). See also Harlow (1977) and Rick Dillingham, Richard W. Lang, and Rain Parrish, *The Red and the Black: Santa Clara Pottery by Margaret Tafoya* (Wheelwright Museum, 1983). The title of this chapter comes from the latter work.

Storytellers and Birds: Middle Rio Grande Pueblos

I am grateful to Barbara Babcock for permission to quote from her many fine publications. Most of the quotes from her interviews with Helen Cordero appear in *The Pueblo Storyteller* by Barbara Babcock and Guy and Doris Monthan (University of Arizona Press, 1986). This book gives a thorough history and survey of figurative potters and pottery. It also has a wonderful bibliography citing other works by Barbara Babcock; see especially "Clay Voices:

Invoking, Mocking, Celebrating," in Victor Turner, ed., *Celebrations* (Smithsonian Institution, 1982).

The story of Clay Old Woman comes from Ruth Benedict's *Tales of the Cochiti Indians* (*Bulletin of the Bureau of American Ethnology* 98, 1931). For Santo Domingo, see Kenneth M. Chapman, *The Pottery of Santo Domingo Pueblo* (University of New Mexico Press, 1953); for Zia, see Michael J. Hering, "The Historic Matte-Paint Pottery of Zia Pueblo, New Mexico, 1680s–1980s," unpublished M.A. thesis, University of New Mexico, 1985.

N. Scott Momaday's book *The Names* (Harper and Row, 1976) has lyrical descriptions of Jemez Pueblo people, landscape, and ceremonies. For a brief description with photographs of Evelyn Vigil's work on Pecos glaze ware, see Sheila Tryk, "Solving the Pecos Pottery Mystery," *New Mexico Magazine*, vol. 57, no. 7 (1979), pp. 20–23. For general overviews of all these pueblos, see Harlow (1977) and Dittert and Plog (1980).

Clay Made From History: Acoma, Laguna, and Zuni

General background on these pueblos appears in Larry Frank and Francis H. Harlow, *Historic Pottery of the Pueblo Indians 1600–1880* (New York Graphic Society, 1974); Harlow (1977); Dittert and Plog (1980); and *Seven Families*. Barbara Moulard's *Within the Underworld Sky: Mimbres Ceramic Art in Context* (Twelvetrees Press, 1984) contains a stimulating text and fine photographs.

For Acoma, see Peterson (1984); and Rick Dillingham's "The Pottery of Acoma Pueblo," *American Indian Art Magazine* (Autumn 1977, pp. 44–51, 84).

The primary source for Zuni is *Gifts of Mother Earth: Ceramics in the Zuni Tradition* by Margaret Ann Hardin (The Heard Museum, 1983). For further detail on the line break, see Kenneth M. Chapman and Bruce T. Ellis, "The Line-Break, Problem Child of Pueblo Pottery," *El Palacio*, vol. 58, no. 9 (1951), pp. 251–289. Josephine Nahohai's owl story comes from Babcock, Monthan, and Monthan (1986).

The Legacy of Sikyatki: Hopi

For Hopi, in addition to the general sources—Dittert and Plog (1980), *Seven Families*, and Harlow (1977)—the best introductory work comes from the Museum of Northern Arizona Press in Flagstaff. See "Hopi and Hopi-Tewa Pottery," *Plateau*, vol. 49, no. 3 (Winter 1977); *An Introduction to Hopi Pottery* by Francis H. Harlow and Katherine Bartlett, 1978; and *Contemporary Hopi Pottery* by Laura Graves Allen, 1984.

Other useful books include Edward Dozier's *Hano: A Tewa Indian Community in Arizona* (Holt, Rinehart and Winston, 1966), for general background; *Hopi Traditions in Pottery and Painting, Honoring Grace Chapella* by John E. Collins (Master's Gallery, 1977); and two books about the beginnings of the Sikyatki revival by Edwin L. Wade and Lea S. McChesney, *America's Great Lost Expedition: The Thomas Keam Collection of Hopi Pottery from the Second Hemenway Expedition, 1890–1894* (The Heard Museum, 1980) and *Historic Hopi Ceramics: The Thomas V. Keam Collection of the Peabody Museum of Archaeology and Ethnology, Harvard University* (Peabody Museum Press, 1981).

One With the Clay: Economics and Tradition

Three articles help here: J. J. Brody, "Pueblo Fine Arts," in the *Handbook of North American Indians*; David Snow, "The Rio Grande Glaze, Matte-Paint and Plainware Tradition," in *Southwestern Ceramics: A Comparative Review* (Arizona Archaeologist, vol. 15, 1982); and also by Snow, "Some Economic Considerations of Historic Rio Grande Pottery," in *The Changing Ways of Southwest Indians: A Historic Perspective*, Albert H. Schroeder, ed. (Rio Grande Press, 1973).

Betty Toulouse, *Pueblo Pottery of the New Mexico Indians: Ever Constant, Ever Changing* (Museum of New Mexico Press, 1977) surveys the history of Pueblo pottery with emphasis on the interaction of potters with museums and Anglo patrons. See also Ralph T. Coe, *Lost and Found Traditions* (University of Washington Press, 1986).

Index

Note: Boldface indicates photographs.

Acoma Pueblo and pottery, 2, 4–6, **11**, 11–12, 14, 19, 23–24, 26, 28, 59, 72–80, **72**, **73**, **75**, **76**, **77**, **78**, **79**, **80**, 81, **103**, 106
Adams, Sadie (Hopi-Tewa), **101**
Anasazi Culture, **x**, 4, 6–7, 73, 77
Applegate, Frank, 93
Archuleta, Mary E. (San Juan-Santa Clara), 20, 23, 25–26, 50–51
Arquero, Juanita (Cochiti), 57
Arquero, Martha (Cochiti), 58
Avanyu, **21**, **39**, **41**, **42**, 43, **44**, **45**; definition of, 39
Awatovi Ruin, 18, 96, 98

Bica family (Zuni), 84
Blue Corn (San Ildefonso), 9, 14, 20, 41–42, **42**
Bunzel, Ruth, 24

Cain, Mary (Santa Clara), 44, **45**, 105
Cata, Regina (San Juan), 51
Chaco Canyon, 6, 73, 77

Chapella, Grace (Hopi-Tewa), 95
Chapman, Kenneth, 77, 79
Chavarria, Stella (Santa Clara), 46–47, **47**
Cheromiah, Evelyn (Laguna), 81
Chino, Grace (Acoma), 74, **76**, 79
Chino, Jodie (Acoma), **11**
Chino, Marie Z. (Acoma), **77**, 79
Clay, 10–14, 42, 52, 74–75, 91, 96–97; definition of, 9; micaceous, 31–33
Cochiti Pueblo and pottery, 4–5, 19, 29, **54**, 55–61, **57**, **59**, **60**, **61**
Concho, Lolita (Acoma), 76
Cordero, Damacia (Cochiti), **59**, 60
Cordero, Helen (Cochiti), 29, 57–58, **57**, 61, 103
Cordero, Tim (Cochiti), 58

Da, Popovi (San Ildefonso), 40–41, 48
Da, Tony (San Ildefonso), 41, 48
Dallas, Tony (Cochiti), 58
Daubs, Glendora (Jemez), **67**
de Herrera, Rosita (San Juan), 51, **52**

de la Cruz, Derek, 10, 37, 48, 104
Denet, Susanna (Hopi), 94–95, 97, 107
Duran, Virginia (Picuris), 24–25, **32**, 32–33, 35
Durand, Cora and Anthony (Picuris), **34**, 35

Fewkes, Jesse Walter, 91–92
Folwell, Jody (Santa Clara), 14, 29, 50
Fragua, Juanita (Jemez), 67–68

Gachupin, Candelaria (Zia), 28, 43, 67
Gachupin, Helen (Zia), 67
Gachupin, Laura (Jemez), 68–69
Garcia, Dolores Lewis (Acoma), 2, 12, 19, 77, 79
Garcia, Goldenrod (Santa Clara-Pojoaque), 48
Garcia, Jessie (Acoma), 78
Garcia, Rose Chino (Acoma), **75**
Girard, Alexander, 57–58
Gonzales, Barbara (San Ildefonso), 12, 20, 41
Gonzales, Rose (San Ildefonso), **41**, 43
Guaco, 55; definition of, 23
Gutierrez, Lela and Van (Santa Clara), 47
Gutierrez, Margaret and Luther (Santa Clara), 47
Gutierrez, Petra (Santa Clara-Pojoaque), 48, 104
Gutierrez, Pula and Val (Santa Clara), 45
Gutierrez, Stephanie (Santa Clara), 47
Gutierrez, Virginia (Nambe-Pojoaque), 12, 25, 48, 52–53, **53**
Gutierrez-de la Cruz, Lois (Santa Clara-Pojoaque), v, vi, **9**, 10, 37, 48, **49**, 104

Hampton, Mary Ann (Acoma), 79
Harlow, Frank, 62
Hering, Michael, 65–66
Herrera, Mary Frances (Cochiti), 58
Hewett, Edgar, 38
Histia, Jackie (Acoma), 24, 75, 78–79, **78**

Hooee, Daisy (Hopi-Tewa), 22–23, 28, 84–85, 87, 92–94, **94**, 100
Hopi Pueblos and Hopi and Hopi-Tewa pottery, 4–7, **8**, 11, **16**, 18, **19**, 20, **22**, 22–25, 28–29, 58, 73–74, 88–101, **88**, **89**, **90**, **92**, **94**, **95**, **96**, **97**, **98**, **99**, **101**, 104, 107
Hopi-Tewa people, 7, 89–90
Hough, Walter, 92
Huma, Rondina (Hopi-Tewa), 28, 95–96, **96**, 98, 100
Huma, Stella (Hopi-Tewa), **90**

Indian Market, Santa Fe, 45, 63, **102**, 104–6
Isleta Pueblo and pottery, 1, 4, 6, 25, 56, 74, 82–83, **83**

Jemez Pueblo and pottery, 4, 6–7, 56, 66–71, **67**, **69**, **70**

Kavena, Rena (Hopi), 9, 14, 25
Kavena, Tracy (Hopi), 9, 14, 23, 25, 96, 100–101
Keam, Thomas, 91–93, 100
Keresan, 5, 7, 55, 73

Laate, Jenny (Acoma-Zuni), **84**, 85
Laguna Pueblo and pottery, 4–7, 11, 19, 24, 73–74, **81**, 81–82
Leno, Juana (Acoma), 12, 74–75, 77, 105–6
Lewis, Dolores. See Garcia, Dolores Lewis
Lewis, Emma. See Mitchell, Emma Lewis
Lewis, Lucy (Acoma), 59, **72**, **73**, 79
Lewis, Nancy (Hopi), **16**
Lewis, Rita and Ivan (Cochiti), **57**, 59, **60**
Line break, **62**, 87, 107
Lockwood, Carnation and Bill (San Juan), 20, 25, 51–52
Lomakema, Lorna (Hopi-Tewa), **101**

Lomaquahu, Percy (Hopi), 104
Lonewolf, Joseph (Santa Clara), 48
Lucario, Rebecca (Acoma), 79, **80**

Martinez, Clara (San Ildefonso), 20, 40
Martinez, Maria and Julian (San Ildefonso), 12, 20, **37**, 38–41, **39**, 44, 58, 91
Martinez, Santana and Adam (San Ildefonso), 11, 13, 25, **37**, **40**, 40–41
Medicine Flower, Grace (Santa Clara), 29, 48
Medina, Elizabeth and Marcellus (Zia), 26, **26–27**, **65**, 65–67
Medina, Sofia and Rafael (Zia), 66–67
Melchor family (Santo Domingo), 62
Mesa Verde, 6, 73, 77
Mimbres Culture and designs, 6, 39, 48, 77, 79–80, **80**, 106
Mitchell, Emma Lewis (Acoma), 14, 19, 22–23, 28, 79
Mogollon Culture, 6–7, 77
Momaday, Al, 68
Momaday, N. Scott, 68
Montoya, Eudora (Santa Ana), 64, **64**

Naha, Helen and Sylvia (Hopi-Tewa), 97–98, **98**
Nahohai, Josephine, Milford, Randy, and Rowena (Zuni), 84–87, **86**, 107
Nambe Pueblo and pottery, 4, 6, 12, 37–38, 52–53, **53**
Namoki, Bessie (Hopi), **8**, 18, **19**, **22**
Nampeyo and Lesou (Hopi-Tewa), 22, 91–95, **92**, 100–101
Nampeyo, Priscilla Namingha (Hopi-Tewa), 100
Naranjo, Rose (Santa Clara), 13, 24, 44–45, 50
Naranjo, Teresita (Santa Clara), **44**
Naranjo, Tito (Santa Clara), 11, 34
Naranjo, Virginia and Louis (Cochiti), 59–61, **61**
Naranjo-Morse, Nora (Santa Clara), 50, **51**, 104–5

Navasie, Joy (Hopi-Tewa), **89**, 97

Ortiz, Seferina (Cochiti), 58

Paquin, Clara (Santa Ana), 64
Paquin, Gladys (Laguna), 14, 19, 24, **81**, 81–82, 105
Pavatea, Garnet (Hopi-Tewa), 97, **97**
Pecos Pueblo and pottery, 7, 70–71, **70**
Peña, Dora Tse Pe (San Ildefonso), 14, **21**, 28–29, 43, 53, 103–104, 107
Peynetsa, Anderson (Zuni), 85
Picuris Pueblo and pottery, 1, 3, 5–6, 11, 25, **31**, 30–35, **32**, **34**
Pino, Lorencita (Tesuque), 53
Pitting problems, 67, 74, 106
Pojoaque Pueblo and pottery, 4, 6, 11–12, 37–38, 48, 52–53, **53**
Pottery, prehistoric, **x**, 6
Potterymaking, techniques of: black pottery, 26, 28, 38, 44; black-on-black decoration, 39; carving, 17, 43, 46, **47**; coiling, 13, **15**; corrugated pottery, 14, 24, 78, **78**, 97; firing, 24–28, **26–27**, 32, 48, 63, 71, 97; glaze paint, 70–71; kilns, electric, 29, 74, 82, 106; molded pottery, 29, 74, 106–7; painting and paints, **22**, 22–24, 66, 68, 70, 77, 87, 91; pinch pot, **8**, 13, 52; polishing, **9**, **18**, 18–20, 45, 47, 68, 98; sanding, **16**, 16–17, 20, 45; sgraffito, 20, **67**; slip, 18–20, **19**, 29, 32–33, 42–43, 48, 56, 58, 63, 91, 96, 98; smoothing, shaping, and scraping, 13–14, **15**; two-tone, resist-fired pots, **21**, 41, 43, 48
Pueblo Indians, 5–6
Puki, definition of, 13

Qoyawayma, Al (Hopi), 100
Qoyawayma, Polingaysi (Elizabeth White) (Hopi), 99, **99**, 103
Quotskuyva, Camille (Hopi-Tewa), 20
Quotskuyva, Dextra (Hopi-Tewa), 2, 10, 14, 20, 22, 29, **88**, 92–94, 101, 103

Rio Grande pueblos, 3–4, 11, 19
Romero, Marie (Jemez), 69
Romero, Virginia T. (Taos), **30**, 32–33

Salvador, Lillian and Wayne (Acoma),
14, 23–24, 74–76, 78, 80, **103**, 104, 106
San Felipe Pueblo and pottery, 4–5, 55,
63, 66
San Ildefonso Pueblo and pottery, 4, 6, 9,
12–13, 20, **21**, 26, 37–43, **37, 39, 40,
41, 42**, 44
San Juan Pueblo and pottery, 4, 6, 25,
37–38, 51–52, **52**, 58
Sanchez, Kathy (San Ildefonso), 41
Sanchez, Russell (San Ildefonso), 43
Sandia Pueblo and pottery, 4, 6, 56, 63
Santa Ana Pueblo and pottery, 4, 5, 56,
64, **64**
Santa Clara Pueblo and pottery, **cover,
frontispiece**, 4, 6, 10, 12–13, **18**, 18–
19, 20, 26, 29, **36**, 37–38, 43–51, **44,
45, 46, 47, 49, 51**
Santo Domingo Pueblo and pottery, 4–5,
15, 19, 22–23, 28–29, 38, 55, 61–63,
62
Sikyatki Ruin, 89, 91, 93, 95, 97, 100
Shije, Eusebia (Zia), **55**, 65–67
Shupla, Helen (Santa Clara), **cover**, vi,
36, 46
Shutiva, Jackie. See Histia, Jackie
Shutiva, Stella (Acoma), 12, 24, 74–75,
78–79, **78**
Storytellers, **57, 60, 61**; definition of, 57
Suazo-Naranjo, Bernice (Taos), 10–12,
17, 17, 22, 25, 28, 34–35, **35**, 105
Suina, Ada (Cochiti), **57**, 58–59

Tafoya, Margaret (Santa Clara), 20, 44,
46
Tafoya, Sarafina and Geronimo (Santa
Clara), 44
Tahbo, Mark (Hopi-Tewa), 13, 95, **95**, 100
Talachy, Thelma (Pojoaque-Santa Clara),
48
Tanoan, 5–6

Taos Pueblo and pottery, 1, 3, **5**, 6, 11–12,
17, 22, **30**, 30–35, **35**, 73
Tapia, Belen and Ernest (Santa Clara),
13, **18**, 20, 45–48
Tapia, Leonidas (San Juan), 58
Teller, Stella, Robin, and Lynette (Isleta),
24–25, 74, 82–83, **83**, 106–7
Temper, 10–12, 64–65, 67–68, 74–75, 82,
96; definition of, 10–11
Tenorio, Robert (Santo Domingo), 13,
15, 19, 22–23, 28–29, **62**, 62–63
Tesuque Pueblo and pottery, 4, 6, 37–38,
53
Tewa Pueblos and pottery, 6, 20, 33, 36–
53, 55
Tiwa, 5–6, 56
Torivio, Dorothy (Acoma), **79**
Torivio, Frances (Acoma), 76
Towa, 6, 7, 56
Toya, Maxine (Jemez), 68–70, **69**
Trujillo, Mary (Cochiti), **54**, 56, 58, 61,
104
Tse-Pe (San Ildefonso), 43
Tse-Pe, Dora. *See* Peña, Dora Tse Pe

Vigil, Evelyn (Jemez), 70–71, **70**
Vigil, Minnie (Santa Clara-Pojoaque), 48
Vigil, Vicenta and Manuel (Tesuque), 53

Western pueblos, 6, 74
White, Elizabeth. *See* Qoyawayma,
Polingaysi

Youngblood, Nathan (Santa Clara), 10,
50
Youngblood-Cutler, Nancy (Santa
Clara), 50
Youvella, Wallace (Hopi), 100

Zia Pueblo and pottery, 4, 5, 11, 23, 26,
26–27, 28, 43, **55**, 56, 63, **65**, 65–68
Zuni Pueblo and pottery, 1, 4–6, 11, 19,
74, **84**, 84–87, **86**, 91